# 5
# SIMPLE WAYS
## TO · TELL
# YOUR CHILD
# "I LOVE
# YOU"

# 52
# SIMPLE WAYS
## TO · TELL
# YOUR CHILD
# "I LOVE
# YOU"

Jan Dargatz

A Division of Thomas Nelson Publishers
NASHVILLE

*Dedicated to*

Johanna
Mary
Kurt, Katelyn, Kiersten
and to all the
children who know me as
"Aunt Jan"

Copyright © 1991 by Jan Dargatz

All rights reserved. Written permission must be secured from the publisher to use or reproduce any part of this book, except for brief quotations in critical reviews or articles.

Published in Nashville, Tennessee, by Oliver-Nelson Books, a division of Thomas Nelson, Inc., Publishers, and distributed in Canada by Lawson Falle, Ltd., Cambridge, Ontario.

Unless otherwise noted, the Bible version used in this publication is THE NEW KING JAMES VERSION. Copyright © 1979, 1980, 1982, Thomas Nelson, Inc., Publishers.

Illustrations of sign language in chapter 6 from *Sign Language for Everyone*, Cathy Rice, copyright 1977 by Thomas Nelson, Inc. Used by permission.

Printed in the United States of America.

Library of Congress Cataloging-in-Publication Data
Dargatz, Jan Lynette.
  52 simple ways to tell your child "I love you" / Jan Dargatz.
    p.    cm.
  ISBN 0-8407-9591-2 (pbk.)
  1. Parent and child.    2. Love.    I. Title.    II. Title: Fifty-two simple ways to tell your child "I love you."
HQ755.85.D37    1991
306.874—dc20                                               91-64716
                                                               CIP

1   2   3   4   5   6—96   95   94   93   92   91

# ✦ Contents

# ✦ Introduction

As common as the phrase "I love" is in our culture, love is not *always* an easy thing to feel. Why? Because loving people requires setting self aside momentarily and focusing our devotion, attention, and affection upon someone other than ourselves. Love is, above all things, unselfish. And most of us are more self-centered than we care to admit.

Still, it is relatively easy to *feel* love compared to how difficult it is for many people to *express* their love. We often find it easier to declare that we "love" a new broccoli recipe or a pair of shoes than to state openly that we love a certain person.

Why is it often difficult for us to express our love? Because love is rooted in giving, and giving is most fulfilling if that which one gives is received. The possibility that someone might not receive what we desire to give makes us vulnerable. Vulnerability carries with it the possibility of rejection, and, in that, embarrassment and an emotional sting. Thus, the greatest, most exhilarating and uplifting emotion we can know also carries within it the potential for the greatest emotional pain. For many people, love goes unexpressed because love carries this risk. These people rarely know great moments of joy, because they fear the possibility of pain.

For others, love goes unstated because the person simply doesn't know how to express the love he or she feels. Perhaps she hasn't been trained in giving or has never been shown love and, therefore, doesn't know how to show it. Perhaps he doesn't know from experience what is most likely to be received and valued as an expression of love. That is where this book can help.

Here are fifty-two ways to show love, to express love in the language that children understand. You will learn to tell your child how you feel with minimal risk and maximal joy.

Many other ways are possible, of course. Let this be just the beginning of your telling your child, "I love *you!*" The good news is that there is no more rewarding enterprise on the face of the earth than to love and be loved by a child.

# 1 ✦ Make a Pledge to Love Your Child

Make *your* love your child's number-one birthright. Count it as the most valuable gift you will ever give your child—greater than your home, greater than any material possessions you might provide, even greater than anything you can teach or show to your child. Your child needs to know that he has your love as an absolute, a given, a known entity in his life.

Let your child know your love is something he can always count on. Admit to your child that there may be times when you don't say you love him—in fact, there may be moments when your child does not even think it to be true—but that, nonetheless, your love is constant.

***Vows of Love*** *"Kiddo, I may not have told you lately, but guess what? It's still true."*

*"What's true?"*

*"The number-one, all-encompassing, never-to-be-denied, absolutely positive fact that I love you."*

Let your child know that your love is not rooted in anything she does, but that you love her simply because she is your child.

*"Honey, I will love you forever."*

*"Son, I will love you always."*

*"Daughter, I love you more than all the universe and everything in it."*

Let your child know that your love for him is a divine gift from God to you for him.

*"God must have loved us a great deal to have blessed us with a son like you."*

*"I just can't help it. God put a great big dose of love in my heart for you, daughter. Nothing can change that. God put it there, and He has assured me that I'm going to have this love for you forever."*

What if you don't feel this spontaneous love for your child? Make that your problem, not your child's. Get help. Seek counsel. Question why you don't love. Face the fact that the problem is within you, not resident in your child. And determine that you *will* love your child. You will get the help you need, you will make loving your child your number-one priority as a parent.

Make a vow of your love. It may be at a reception after the christening, baptism, or dedication of your child. It may be in the form of a toast at a family dinner. Don't just feel your pledge of love—declare it. Confess it to others. Speak it. Put it into words. Make it a declaration in time and space. Ask other family members to support you in your pledge to love your child. Don't keep your vow a secret from your child. Let your child know that you have made a pledge to love him always.

**Certificates of Love**    One way to express your love for your child is to declare your child's birthright of love with a "Love Certificate" of some type. One couple added this line to their child's birth certificate: "Conceived in love, birthed with love, and with God's help, nurtured to adulthood by love."

Another couple wrote out a "Parents' Pledge" to their children. They worked on the statement together during the pregnancy of their first child, had a calligrapher write it out beautifully, and then had a copy of it framed for each child's room. The statement concludes, "The best birthright we can give you is our love. Our love is our blessing on your life. Our love is your assurance that you have never been and will never be a mistake in our eyes. Our love is the most precious gift we can give you—and we give it freely because you are the most precious gift ever given to us!"

One mother worked the message into a birth-record piece of cross-stitched embroidery: "7 pounds and 1 ounce of pure love."

One father wore a T-shirt with this message on the front: "Go ahead. Make my day. Ask me how much I love my children."

Your love is the best gift you can ever give your child. More than anything else, your love gives your child a feeling of security, a foundation for healthy self-esteem, and good mental and emotional health throughout his or her life.

# 2 ✦ Meet Your Child's Basic Needs

Before your child can ever truly believe you when you say "I love you," your child must know that you are vitally concerned about meeting his or her basic needs. These needs include nourishment, shelter, and safety.

***Nourishment*** Children need nutritional foods prepared in nutritional ways. They need pure drinking water. "But my children don't like certain foods," you may say. Train them to like them. Serve a wide variety of foods. Prepare them in the simplest ways possible: raw, steamed, baked, broiled. Let children experience the fullness of flavors without layers of salt, chemical preservatives, or oils.

Children's minds also require nourishment. Children need exposure to a wide variety of stimuli that will trigger their creativity, spark their imaginations, and promote their developing sense of values. They need experiences more than they need toys. They need play time more than they need media time. They need opportunities for relating with other children and adults.

This does not mean that you need to overload your child with flashcards and schooling at an early age or that you need to create a toy-store atmosphere in your child's room. To a child, the cupboard with pots and pans holds great creative potential. The backyard can be jungle, forest, or beach—the back porch a fortress, palace, or dungeon. The opportunity to be with you in the kitchen as you prepare a meal may be the best lesson of the day.

- Ask yourself, "Does the toy I'm providing stimulate creativity?
- Ask yourself, "Does this activity promote the values and mental growth that I want to see in my child?"

**Shelter** *Children also need shelter.* As a basic need, they require protection from the harshness of their environment. A child's environment encompasses more than the weather.

Mothers who would never dream of sending their children out to play in the snow without mittens and hats often fail to see a threat in the constant din of noise outside their city window. Children need quiet. They need to know that they can shut off and shut out the world.

Children need warmth when it is cold and cool shelter from the heat. They need to be able to get into their own homes using door latches that are within reach and doors that they can open easily. They need to be able to get to a glass of cold water without asking for permission or help. They need to be able to take off a layer of clothing or add a layer.

Children need space. They need to have a corner of the world they can *call* their own, in which they are free to create a world *of* their own. For some, it may be a bed of their own. For others, it may be a room of their own, the bottom of a small closet, or a treehouse.

*Safety*   Children need freedom from pain. They need to know that their parents are doing everything possible to keep them healthy. One of the best ways to be sure you are meeting your child's basic needs is to make regular trips to a pediatrician. Have your child's hearing and eyesight checked periodically. Regular dental care also falls into this category.

Children also need freedom from emotional and mental pain. They need to be sheltered from abusive situations.

Note that the emphasis here is on needs, not wants. You do *not* have a responsibility to provide for all of your child's *wants*. You do *not* have a responsibility to provide the best, most elaborate products, services, or environment possible. A modest house can be just as much a home as a mansion. A pair of jeans wears just as well *without* a designer label.

The root of love is not emotion, it is provision. By providing for your child's basic needs, you are establishing a foundation on which love has meaning. Meet your child's basic needs, and your expressions of love will be all your child ever needs in addition.

# 3 ✦ Nicknames

A nickname, a term of endearment, is one of the easiest ways to express your love to your child on a daily basis. For my brother and me, the names were simply "Jannie" and "Craigie." The names look strange in print, but they never sounded strange to our ears. They were what Mommy and Daddy called us.

Nicknames—special, affectionate, private names—are a wonderful bonding device when they are used in a loving way.

*Make a nickname an endearing signal of a loving relationship unique to your child.* Don't call anyone else by that name. A nickname says to a child, "You're extra special to me. I have a name for you that embodies my love. It's a name I use *only* for you!"

**Privacy** *A loving nickname is best used in privacy.* It is almost as good as a secret code name. It says to the world, "There's a relationship here that's private and closed to the outside world."

- Always make certain that your child is comfortable with the nickname.

  When possible, adopt something of the child's

initial choosing, perhaps something they called themselves or by which they have identified themselves. You might ask your child, "Who are you to me?" (This question can be a revealing one on many levels. Be prepared for an eye-opening answer.)

• Don't use a nickname that embarrasses your child either personally or in public.

Avoid nicknames that refer to physical traits or family standing. The child nicknamed "Baby" won't like that nickname once he has grown to be six feet tall and starts to shave. "Junior" describes a relationship; it is not a true nickname. And no child wants to be called "Boopsie" once she hits puberty. If a child says, "Don't call me *that*" . . . then, don't.

**Continuity**   Nicknames used over the months and years give a child a sense of consistency in a relationship. I was Jannie forty years ago. I'm still Jannie today. My nickname suggests continuity, long-standing affection, and a sense of confidence that "I'm sombody" on the inside, even if the outside world never knows it.

A nickname used over the years and decades becomes a synonym for "unique and wonderful." And in that, there's love!

# 4 ✦ Read with Your Child

One of the easiest and most cherished ways of spending time with your child is to read with your child. Reading together creates a closed unit. For those few minutes in a day, your child knows that she has your undivided attention. She also knows, as she sits close to you or on your lap, that the two of you are virtually impervious to outside demands.

***Read Aloud to Your Child*** Even when your child is still in the crib, read! Let your child experience the way that you put words together, the inflections that you use, the different character voices that you adopt. Let your child delight in a variety of stories. Choose books for your young child that trigger his or her imagination.

As your child grows older, let your child help with the choosing. Make visits to the library a regular part of your family routine.

Here are some pointers for reading together:

- Hold your child close. Let him know that you are not only eager to share mind to mind, but that you desire to be in close proximity.
- Personalize a story whenever you can. Point out

things in illustrations that may not be a part of the story. Ask your child questions: *"What do you think will happen next?" "Which one of these do you like best?" "Have you ever felt this way?"*

- Move at a pace that is comfortable to your child. She will let you know when you are going too fast or too slow. Stopping you from turning a page means, "Not so fast, Dad. Slow down. I need more time with this page—and with you." Fidgeting means, "Read faster, Mom." Flipping ahead to the next page means, "I don't have enough attention span to listen to all of this. Cut to the chase."

***Let Your Child Read Aloud to You***    Value what your child reads to you. Listen attentively. Sit side by side. Ask questions when they seem appropriate, but stop asking if your child reprimands you for interrupting. Don't fret over words read incorrectly. Help your child with words only if he asks for your help. He's looking for love, not education.

One young father I know wanted to have a reading time with his children but, as a farmer who was up and at work by 4 A.M., he was often too tired to stay awake beyond the first few pages of a story. He finally resorted to stories on tape. He would lie on one of the children's beds with the tape deck on his stomach and a child tucked under each arm. Together, they listened to tales serious and humorous. A few times his children had to awaken him to have him turn over the tape, but these reading sessions were filled with love and closeness.

Make reading times a regular part of your daily schedule.

- Capture a few moments while dinner is cooking to sit down with your child and read. Reading is a great way to help a child unwind from play and settle down for a quiet evening.
- You may want to read with your child after bath-time and before bedtime, as a cozy transition toward a peaceful night.

Bear in mind that just as your child is never too young for a reading time, so your child is never too old. Your teenager might not sit as close to you, but you can still enjoy the intimacy of a story shared together.

As your children grow older, have nights when the living room becomes a reading room—with every-body reading. Be willing to be interrupted by a child who finds a passage too humorous to keep to him-self. Be willing to share what you find to be of special interest.

Books provide fertile ground for parent-child relationships. And in that ground, love grows exceedingly well.

# 5 ✦ Make Something Together

Your child will always understand love expressed in terms of time spent together. One of the best ways of spending time together is to make something together.

The point of the exercise is this: do it *together*. Don't choose an activity in which you are doing the making and your child is doing the watching. Also avoid activities in which your child is doing the making and you are doing the supervising.

**Things to Do** What are some good things to do together? Here are four neutral, evenly shared activities for you to consider.

*Cooking.* You chop up one ingredient. Let your child chop up another. You make the cake. Let your child make the frosting. You make the meat dish. Let your child make the salad. You turn the crank for homemade ice cream. Let your child watch the meat on the grill.

*Gardening.* You plant one row. Let your child plant the adjacent row. You weed one patch. Let your child weed another. You pick the tomatoes. Let your child harvest the zucchini.

*Doing jigsaw puzzles.* Work on one part of the puzzle as your child works on another. You find a piece; your child finds a piece.

*Making models.* (This includes dollhouses, birdhouses, train sets, and so forth.) You paint some of the pieces. Let your child paint the others. Paper one wall of the dollhouse while your child papers another. Hold pieces for each other while the glue sets.

### How to Work Together   In working together, follow a few simple rules to keep the activity loving and not confrontational.

- *Be willing to accept your child's work.* Allow for imperfections. Be willing for the carrot slices to be of varying thickness. Be willing for the glue to ooze out around some pieces.
- *Choose something that you both regard as important or fun.* Don't insist that your child build a model airplane when he would rather be putting together a model ship. Let your child help choose the puzzle and help decide what to do with it after it is finished (such as frame it, pull it apart, give it away, make a mosaic-style tray out of it).
- *Whenever possible, choose activities that don't have a deadline or a tight time frame.* Make this a relaxed time to be together. If a child feels the pressure of time, he is likely to make even more mistakes than he might normally, which will make the activity less fun for him. Don't expect your child to be as quick as you are at a task.

- *Don't make this activity an excuse for conversation.* Many parents choose to do something with their child as a way of starting a conversation or in hopes that their child will open up to them on an important topic. Your child may; she may not.
- *Praise your child for the work he does.* Let him know you value his effort, his skill, his accomplishment. *"Good job." "Thanks." "You know, we're really getting good at this."*
- *Let your child know you are happy to be with him.* Say, *"You know, I'd rather be doing this with you than just about anybody I can think of." "I like digging potatoes with you." "You're a good sport to be doing this with me."*
- *Choose an activity that has an end.* Dinner eventually gets on the table. The gardening is eventually over for the day or the season. The puzzle gets finished. The glue dries and the model is put up on the shelf. The dollhouse is finally finished and ready for play.

The beauty or success of the thing you have made is not what your child will remember or praise. The time that you have spent together and the fact that you have made something together are what will be remembered as examples of your love shared.

# 6 ✦ Sign Language

Learn to say "I love you" in your own personal sign language. That way, you can send your message even across a crowded room.

In the language of the deaf, "I love you" is generally expressed in these three hand motions:

Point to yourself.      Cross your heart.      Point to the other person.

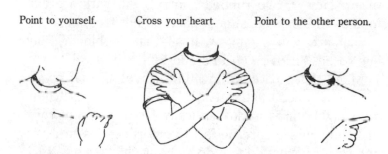

***Private Messages***   You don't need to use large motions to convey the message, however. There are times when you should "whisper" your message, even when using signals. Be discreet and aware of your child's reactions. You can always point to your heart and cross it with just a finger and then nod to the other person with a wink. That's the way one mother sent encouragement to her children as they were up on stage preparing to sing a song in the church Christmas pageant.

***Creative Messages*** Encourage your child to be creative in the ways he expresses the "I love you" message. One young boy I know pointed to his mouth instead of to his heart. He then grinned broadly, all of his front teeth showing, and held his finger up closely to his mouth to point at his grandfather. In his own sign language, he was probably conveying, "I smile you" or "I grin you." In truth, he was saying, "I love you, Grandpa!"

Another young child rubbed her heart area instead of crossing it. She rubbed and rubbed, with a great look of seriousness, almost pain, on her face. I asked, "What are you saying with all that rubbing?" She answered, "I love you lots and lots and *lots.*"

Many times parents find themselves too far away to give an encouraging word. What do you say when your child stares back frantically from the front row just moments before he is to perform in his first piano recital? What do you do as your child prepares to march onto the football field in her first appearance as a majorette?

Use sign language. Others may be able to "overhear" what you say, but nobody will be embarrassed by your message, including your child.

# 7 ✦ Keep Your Child's Secrets

Love is based on trust. Your child must be able to trust your words as being true. Your child must be able to trust that you are *always* concerned that his needs are met. Your child must be able to trust that you will *always* be her ally.

Your child's trust can be gained, in part, by keeping your child's secrets. On the other hand, nothing can destroy your child's trust in you faster than by your betraying his confidence.

Must you keep all of your child's secrets? Yes. You do, however, have the prerogative of defining what a secret may or may *not* be.

## When Secrets Are Something Else

Share with your child the difference between a piece of information and a secret. Only allow your child to classify as secrets those things that are about himself and himself alone. You cannot and must not be responsible for secrets about other children.

Teach your child the difference between telling a secret and making an admission of guilt. Just because your child tells you something and says that it is in confidence doesn't mean that he can't be punished for it. "If I tell you a secret, will you promise not to be mad, Mom?" asks your child. Don't agree! You may be stuck with an admission such as, "I just picked all the daisies in Mrs. Smith's yard."

**When Secrets Are Implied**  Many of the things your child does should also be considered a secret by you, even if that word is never used or your child doesn't ask you to keep something a secret. The world doesn't need to know when your daughter starts wearing a bra. The entire neighborhood doesn't need to hear from you that your son just kissed a girlfriend for the first time.

Even your best friend doesn't need to know the intimate conversations you may have with your child about his problems, her questions, his fears, her decisions.

Children retell their own secrets. Don't be surprised to discover that you aren't the only one who has been told something in the highest confidence. Very often, a child will tell you something as a secret only to see how you will react, what you will say, and to test the waters of adult opinion on a subject, incident, or idea.

By keeping your child's secrets in confidence, you are saying, "Your trust is precious to me, so precious I won't willingly do anything to destroy it." Trust creates an atmosphere in which love is freely expressed and freely received; it is the atmosphere in which the words "I love you" are spoken with the greatest validity.

# 8 ✦ Require Honesty of Feelings

Don't cover up your feelings. Don't allow your child to cover up his. When you are angry or disappointed or hurt, say so. When you are happy, excited, or satisfied, say so.

A child who hears honest emotions from an adult comes to appreciate honest emotions and is more willing to express them. Why is honesty of emotions important? Because you want your child to believe you when you express your deepest, highest, and ultimate emotion: "I have a heart bursting with love for you!"

**Personhood Versus Deeds**   Emotional reactions are generally very specific reactions to what someone has said or done. It is important for your child to hear you make a distinction between how you feel about a person and how you feel about that person's behavior in a specific instance.

- "I'm so happy that I got a raise. This means that my boss is happy with my work, and I like knowing that I'm doing a good job. This also means that we'll have a little more money to spend. I like that fact, too!"

- "I'm really disappointed that I didn't get to go on the trip. I was looking forward to seeing London. But I realize that Daddy had to go alone this time and that it was a work trip, not a vacation."
- "I'm very angry that you picked all of Mrs. Smith's flowers. That was a mean and naughty thing to do. I want you to go to your room, and I'll be in shortly to punish you."

By making statements such as these you are separating your feelings about certain actions, decisions, or behavior from the personhood of your boss, your husband, or your child.

What would be the result, however, if one said, *"I'm so happy. I've got the greatest boss in the world."* The implication is that the boss is the cause of happiness. Your child doesn't know what the boss did to cause your happiness, only that your boss and happiness are related. An emotion becomes linked to a person, not to that person's behavior.

*"I'm so disappointed. Daddy gets to go and I don't."* The implication is that Daddy is responsible for the disappointment. Daddy is so closely linked to disappointment that it is not a far reach for a child to conclude that Daddy is a disappointment.

*"I'm so angry. You are a naughty boy."* The action isn't separated from the child. Naughty now? Naughty always? Naughty for this? Or, naughty as a character trait?

It is important for your child to know that you love

him for *who he is,* even though you may not always like *what he does.* Otherwise, your love becomes deed-bound. Your child will forever be trying to earn your love or win your love. He will feel he must *do* something to deserve your love or be worthy of your love. A child needs to know that he *has* your love and your devotion but that his *deeds* may, at times, have your disapproval.

Only as your child understands that deeds and personhood are separate will he be able to differentiate punishment for deeds from punishment for character. If your child knows he is being punished for his misdeeds, he can learn to change those deeds—which is the reason for punishment in the first place.

## Love Versus Qualifications for Love

Tell your child what you like about other people. But keep love separate from qualifications whenever possible.

*"I love you because you are my son. That's the most special love in the world. There's nothing like it. It just is. I love you because of who you are."*

*"I love you because you are my daughter. You're one of a kind and totally unique to me, and my love for you isn't like anything I've ever felt for anyone else. I love you just because you are you."*

Those statements will be perceived as honest ones only if you are honest about the way you feel at other times. Give your child words and emotions he can trust.

# 9 ✦ Freely Forgive

Nothing frees a child more to experience your love than for you to forgive your child. Children know at a fairly early age when they have done something to earn their parents' disapproval.

*Sin* is a serious word, not one to be taken lightly. It is important for you to discuss with your child the difference between *sins* and *mistakes.*

**Mistakes**  Mistakes are things your child does accidentally in the course of trying to do right or good things. Mistakes also are made when children don't focus their attention on what they are doing, when they are trying to do something for the first time and as they practice a skill. Mistakes are often made in the course of a child's seeking to have fun.

The new shoes are ruined as the result of the child's stomping through too many puddles. The glass of milk is knocked over as the child, trying to be independent, reaches for the bowl of olives. The skirt is ripped as the child climbs over a fence in an effort to get home on time.

Mistakes generally result in some type of damage to people or things or events. Sins, on the other hand, are those willful acts that breach or cause damage to a relationship.

**Sins**   Unrepented and unforgiven sins shut down communication, destroy trust, cause guilt, and, ultimately, create a false sense of reality in the child's mind.

*Lying, cheating (and other acts of dishonesty),* and *stealing* are common childhood sins. Indeed, children seem to have an inbred ability to commit them from toddlerhood on.

The problem with sins is that they compound. One sinful act tends to breed another. What's a parent to do?

- *It is the responsibility of the parent to confront the child with his sins.* Mistakes are generally obvious to all, and confrontation is rarely necessary. Sins are often more subtle. Let your child know that you know that he has done something to breach your trust and to muddy the waters of your communication and the close loving relationship that you value dearly.
- *It is the responsibility of the parent to hear the child's full confession.* Don't react too quickly. Make sure you hear the whole story. Don't allow your child to confess only half of what he did or admit to only half of what she didn't do. Don't move toward punishment too quickly. Hear your child out. Look for underlying motives. Probe a little.

- *It is the responsibility of the parent to punish sin.*
  Sin has consequences. That is part of what
  makes it sin. If the consequences don't come
  from you at an early age, they will come from
  someone else at some other time, and usually
  with far more severity.

  Mistakes are also punishable, especially for
  acts in which the child has been forewarned (and
  thus, the mistake is an act of disobedience) or
  for acts in which the error could have been
  avoided by forethought. Punishment is a means
  of training a child not to do certain deeds again.
  Punishments for mistakes, however, can generally be less severe than those administered for
  sin because mistakes are generally more quickly
  recognized.

  What type of punishment is best? Simply put,
  a punishment should be something your child
  doesn't want. There is no perfect punishment
  that works for all children. It may be a spanking.
  It may be foregoing a planned outing.
- *It is the parent's responsibility to forgive the child.*
  Punishment is aimed at the deed of the child.
  Forgiveness is aimed at the guilt and the stain
  on the relationship.

Don't wink at your child's sins. Give your child the
freedom of spirit that comes through confrontation,
repentance, an appropriate punishment, and your
freely given forgiveness. That says to a child, "I love
you enough to care about who you become."

# 10 ✦ Let Your Child Know You Didn't Make a Mistake

Children need to feel wanted in order for them to feel truly loved. Very often, children draw a conclusion from a parent's momentary indifference or temporary neglect that Mommy doesn't want me around or that Daddy doesn't care if I live or die.

Your young child lives in the moment and from moment to moment. He can hear from you five times a day that you love him and he won't grow tired of it.

As your child grows older, he requires less frequent telling. Your relationship has more time built into it. Trust runs deeper. He is more sure of your presence and your love.

Nevertheless, it is important periodically to assure your child that she is wanted, that you wouldn't trade her for the world (and several planets and stars), and that you don't even like to think about how drab life would be without her.

One of the most cherished letters I ever received from my mother was one in which she described an afternoon ride she and my father had taken up into the mountains. They had spent several hours exploring this road and that one. Mom wrote, "We talked about whether we would do it all over again if we knew then what we know now, and we decided that, yes, we would." By "doing it all over again" she was referring to their marriage and their decision to have children. Even at age twenty-two, I felt a warm glow in reading her letter. I had never suspected that I was unwanted. In fact, I was quite sure during all my growing-up years that I had been very much wanted as a baby and that I was very much wanted, appreciated, and loved as a child. Still, it was nice to have it confirmed one more time.

- Tell your child that you are glad he was born. Convey to your child, *"I'm glad you're alive. I'm glad you're you. I'm glad you're here."*
- Let your son know that you are glad he was born *your son.* Let your daughter know that you are glad she was born *your daughter.*
- Let your adopted child know that if you had to do the choosing again, you would make the same choice.
- Let your child know he was an answer to prayer, that she was your heart's desire.

Give your child the assurance that you have wanted him, you do want him, and that you will always want him. That is the best foundation for love that you can establish.

# 11 ✦ Keep a Special Place for Memories of Your Child

Have a special place where you keep photos and other momentos about your child. Have a special place, too, where you record your feelings and memories about your child. Let your child know that he is so precious to you that you want to cherish every minute of his life.

Your special place may be . . .

- a drawer.
- a cupboard.
- a large wooden box.
- a trunk or chest.
- an album, journal, or scrapbook.

Ellen kept a journal during her pregnancy to record, on a periodic basis, how she was feeling about the child developing within her womb. She wrote about how she felt when she first heard the news that she was pregnant and about how excited she was the day she heard the baby's heartbeat. She told about how she felt the first time the baby kicked inside her. After her son was born, she wrote in great detail about her feelings, the reactions of his father and grandparents, and her hopes and dreams for her child, that he might grow up to be a loving, generous, sensitive man.

Jerry wrote about life with his toddler, Rachel, in a small book he titled simply, "Rachel of Heather Cottage"—Heather Cottage being the name they had given to their home. He wrote about the funny things she did and said and about his feelings as a father during those early growing-up years. What a gift beyond price to Rachel.

**Things to Do**   Write little notes alongside the photos in your album telling something about the events, special memories, and feelings.

Keep your child's love notes. Tuck them into your Bible or into a box designated just for that purpose.

Keep sample Christmas cards, especially the ones with photos of your children on them, for each of your children's scrapbooks.

## Love Means Being a Pack Rat    Your
child equates his things with himself. "Mine!" must certainly be one of the Top Ten First Words every child learns. When your child sees you valuing his things—his little drawings, his notes, his awards, his newspaper clippings, photos of himself—he begins to believe, "Mom loves my stuff. Mom loves me. Daddy is proud of my creations and accomplishments. Daddy is proud of me."

# 12 ✦ Get Down on Your Child's Level

Stoop. Kneel. Crawl. Sit. Lie down on the floor. Do whatever it takes to get down on your child's level at least once a day. You will discover a number of things as you see the world through your child's eyes.

## *New Discoveries*

- *You'll realize how big and how frightening some things can be.* Close your eyes and imagine how big your dining table would have to be if it was built in proportion to your *present* height.

  Imagine staring a dog in the eye and knowing that he weighs twice as much as you do and has four legs instead of your two.

  Imagine staring up at an angry person who is more than twice your height and having that person wave in your direction a wooden spoon that is half your height.

  Imagine sitting atop a ten-foot stool. That is proportionately how your child feels as he sits in his high chair. It's a long way down to that floor.

- *You'll realize what an incomplete view your child has of the world.* One year I decided to take a young friend out for a look at the Christmas lights in our city, only to realize after he was all buckled into the front seat of my little red car that he couldn't see out the windows!

Your child may be able to look up and see the stained glass windows as you sit together in church. He may be able to look around and see bodies of adults. But chances are, he can't see the preacher or the altar.

I recently took a couple of young friends to a children's theater performance. The audience was enthusiastic, the play exciting, and the standing ovation given at the conclusion of the final act a rousing one. Suddenly I felt a tug at my skirt and heard three mournful words: "I can't see!"

- *You'll realize how unstimulating much of the world seems with all of the "good stuff" placed way too high.* Imagine a world that looks like the front of your sofa, the edge of the bed, the lower half of your kitchen cabinets, or the enamel of your kitchen appliances.

    Paintings are nearly always hung too high for a young child to enjoy them. The prettiest and most enticing things are nearly always "up there" out of reach.

- *You'll realize how out of control you really are as a child.* Faucets and door knobs and door bells are all out of reach. Toilets are too big. Clothes are hung on closet rods that are too high. In order to get or do many of the essential things in life, you've got to have help. Crawl around in your child's world for awhile, and you will have a new appreciation for some of his frustrations and fears.

**New Opportunities**  With your new awareness of how your child sees his or her environment, you will have new opportunities to stimulate your child's creativity. Take time to point out some things to your child. Help him notice things you would like for him to recognize in his world.

Take some props from the upper world down to your child's level with you. Let your child feel and hold items as he sits three inches from the floor. This not only gives your child a sense of control and encourages his creativity, but there is less chance the item will break if it is dropped.

You will have a new opportunity to play with your child. Let your child know that you can have fun in her world, just as you anticipate that she will have fun in yours. You will have a new opportunity to tell your child, "I love you."

There is no more effective way of telling your child "I love you" than by telling him eye-to-eye. Often we pull children up to our level. We lift them up on our laps or into our arms or let them stand on their bed to tell them we love them. Try getting down on your child's level and telling him from that vantage point. He will *know* you mean it.

# 13 ✦ Find Something to Do for Mutual Fun

Find something to do with your child that you *both* enjoy doing. And then spend time with your child doing that thing. Fun with you and time with you— your child will feel a double dose of love.

**Key Ingredients** There are five key ingredients for having a successful fun time with your child.

- *Make certain the activity is something you both enjoy doing.* If you are doing something only because your child enjoys it, you'll get tired of it easily and you won't want to do it. The result is that you won't do it or you will resent doing it. The same holds true for your child.
- *Make certain the activity is not something that you enable your child to do but that you truly both do.* Don't just hold the jumprope so your son can jump. Don't look over your daughter's shoulder while she takes on Ms. PacMan at the video arcade. Don't just watch while your child rides the carousel.
- *Make certain that the activity doesn't hurt either*

*one of you, physically or emotionally.* When children and adults play tag football together, guess who most often gets hurt? When you carry a child on your shoulders the length of the entire mall, guess who has the sore neck?

Parents often find themselves competing with their children as they play with them. It may be inadvertent or subconcious. It is competition, nonetheless. Children don't enjoy losing or being embarrassed any more than adults do. If you are going to play a competitive game with your child, make sure it is a game in which your child (with a fairly high percentage of probability) can win.

• *Don't get locked into an activity. Stay flexible with it.* Watch your child at play with his peers. They can move from one game to the next with hardly a blink of the eye. They can play out a dozen different scenarios in the course of an afternoon at the park. Children frequently don't finish a board game or play all the innings. Don't insist that your child finish every game you begin. (Insist sometimes, not all the time.)

Don't insist that your child always play by the rules. Children like to make up their own rules. Of course, you may insist that once they make up the rules, they don't change them midstream. At the same time, recognize that very few games have rules that can't be altered.

• *Find an activity that gives you room to laugh.* Having fun with your child is a *process,* not an accomplishment. Fun is marked by laughter, a sense of play, a delight in the doing. Fun is marked by pleasure. If you or your child can't laugh along the way, and if you feel no pleasure in the sheer act of *doing* something, don't do it. It's just not fun.

**What to Do**   So what can you do with your child that is fun, enjoyed mutually, not harmful to either one of you, and which you can both do without a time frame or omnipresent goal? Ask your child! You can say to your child, "Tell me the top ten things you like to do most in the whole world."

Chances are, there will be at least one of your child's Top Ten Things to Do that you like to do or think you might like to try. If not, ask your child for another batch of things she likes to do. Even if you settle for the eighteenth activity on her list, you may be surprised that by doing it together, and having fun together, that activity quickly moves into your child's Top Ten.

It is your time, your attention, and your laughter shared only with him that your child craves. A mutually enjoyed and mutually exclusive time together is a surefire way of saying, "I want to be with you. I love you."

# 14 ✦ Just Say So

Gather up all your courage. Take the time. Find a private moment. And mean it when you say it. But most importantly, give voice to the words "I love you."

## It's Not Always Easy

- *Sometimes it takes courage to tell a child you love him.* The older a child grows, the more many parents feel the potential for their child to reject them. A shrug of the shoulders from a teen hurts just as much as from a spouse or a boss or a pastor. Rejection is rejection is rejection. That's the time when you need to muster your courage. Say, "I love you" even if you get a bad reaction or no reaction.
- *Telling your child you love him takes time and privacy.* A casually tossed, "I love you" will be perceived as a casually tossed emotion.

    Don't try to tell your child you love him when he is with his friends—or with anybody else, for that matter. Find a private moment.

    Find a moment when your statement isn't linked to anything your child has won or earned.

Saying "I love you" after your child is named class president sends a subtle message to your child, "Dad loves me *because* I'm class president." Your child needs to know that you love him because he is your son and for no other reason.

- *Mean it when you say it.* Your child has built-in radar for insincerity. Your child knows when your words ring with a hollow sound.

You may not feel a great emotional surge in saying "I love you" to your child. Many times emotions run deeper than words.

### Love Is for Always

Always keep in mind that love is more than a feeling. It is a declaration of your will, your desire, your state of being quite apart from your emotions. Emotions tend to be rooted in "now." Love is rooted in "always." You can *mean* something, even if you don't feel your heart jumping hurdles. Don't confuse the feeling of love with the *fact* of love. Assure your child that you love him as a undeniable, irrefutable, unchangeable fact of your life.

Don't assume that your child is so confident of your love that he will be annoyed at your saying the words. No child ever gets tired of hearing "I love you" from a parent who means what he says and who chooses the right time and place to say so.

# 15 ✦ Give Thanks for Your Child in Times of Prayer

Pray for your child. Let your child hear your thanksgiving to God for him or her. Nothing conveys a more intimate or deeper sense of your love.

"God loves you and I do, too." That is a good thought to convey to your child often. Confirm that truth for both God and your child to hear.

> *Thank you, Lord, for sending Jessica to our family to be our daughter. We know that she is Your precious child and she is our precious child, too.*

Thank God for the many wonderful traits of your child.

> *Heavenly Father, we're so grateful that You have sent Billy to be a part of our family. We marvel every day at the way in which You have created him.*

Thank God for your child's accomplishments.

> *Thank You, Lord, for helping Paul to score two goals in his soccer game today. Thank You for*

*giving him such a strong body and the energy to run and play so well.*

Thank God for your child's acts of courage and moral bravery.

*Heavenly Father, I thank You that You helped Kirsten to do what was right today, to tell the truth even though it was hard to do. Thank You for giving her the courage not to tell a lie.*

Thank God for your child's friends, teachers, and family members.

*Thank you, heavenly Father, for giving Colton such a good T-ball coach and for giving him friends to play ball with. Thank You, too, for letting Joe's nursery sponsor the team.*

*Lord, we're grateful that Aunt Sue can come visit us for a few days. Please give her a safe trip and help us to have a good time with her while she's here. We know she loves us all. Help us to show her how much we love her. Thank you that she is our Aunt Sue.*

Thank God for protecting your child and for giving her health.

*Father, thank You for keeping Carolina safe as she played today. Thank You for giving her such good health. Thank You for helping her remember to brush her teeth without my having to remind her.*

You can't always be with your child. And no parent knows how many days, months, or years she has with her child. Keep your child's heart open to receiving God's love.

Ask God to help your child with his or her problems and needs.

*Lord God, I ask You tonight to help Tammi know what to do and what to say to her friend Brenda. Give her the courage to speak up and to be able to tell Brenda how she feels about Brenda's rebellious attitude toward her parents.*

In your times of prayer with your child, ask God to help you be a loving parent.

*Heavenly Father, thank You for letting Carla be our daughter. Help me to be a good parent to her. Help me to find new ways to show her how much I love her and appreciate her.*

Finally, give your child an opportunity to pray for you. When you are down or facing a problem at work or are feeling ill or are tired, ask your child to pray for you. Let your child know that her prayers count.

Prayer times with your child may well be the most intimate times you will ever share with your child. Make the most of them in conveying your love and God's love to your child.

# 16 ✦ Hugs and Kisses

Nearly every child loves to be hugged and kissed, even if he won't admit it. Hugs and kisses are an important way to express your love to your child.

Try letting your child—or teen—know that you need a hug. You may be surprised at how willing he is to give one to you!

Hugs and kisses convey to your child that you appreciate his or her physical personhood. Young children see themselves in terms of their bodies. They don't yet have a well-developed concept of their own minds or spirits, although they certainly use them and operate out of them. They do know, however, that they have toes and arms.

Some parents wonder just how much of a hug to give. Here are some simple rules:

- Let the child hug *you* as much as you hug him. Don't hug your child beyond what he or she is comfortable hugging you back.

  Some children are clingers. They can drape themselves around your neck for fifteen minutes and they never seem to grow tired of being held. Other children are blitzers. They are willing to hug you for all of five seconds and then they are off to their next activity. (Blitzers do often come around for a dozen five-second hugs, however.) Don't try to cling to a blitzer, and don't try to blitz a clinger.

- Be aware of each child's need, mood, and means of expressing his love to you.

  Don't insist on hugging a child if she doesn't want to be hugged. If the child says no—either in words or body language—accept that as her mood of the moment and respond simply, "Well, maybe later." Don't force a hug.

- Keep kisses light and playful.

  Should you kiss a child on the mouth? Probably not, unless it's your own son or daughter. And then, only if your child is comfortable with that kind of kiss. Children will often spontaneously kiss you with a giant, slobbery on-the-mouth variety. Accept that with a "Wow, what did I do to deserve that" attitude.

- When a child hits puberty, shift to shoulder hugs. Or wrap your arms around your child's shoulders or waist from the back as he or she is slouching in the sofa or sitting on a bench.

Above all, keep your hugging and kissing innocent and not insistent, but keep those hugs and kisses coming. Your child needs to know, always, as a primary need, that you like his physical personhood. A child whose parents reject his or her body as untouchable will have a difficult time hearing their words, "I love you."

# 17 ✦ Give Flowers to Your Child

The giving of flowers conveys a strong message of love, in our culture and in that of many others. Flowers can express

- *love in times of celebration.*
- *love in the depths of grief.*
- *love in terms of appreciation.*

Give your child flowers from an early age. He or she will look back later and say, "Hmmm . . . flowers mean love in this world. Mom and Dad always gave them to me. Mom and Dad loved me then and love me now."

Give flowers to both your son and daughter. Don't discriminate. Glenda once said to her teenage son when she spontaneously brought home a bouquet of daisies to him: "This is an example of 'do unto others as you would have them do unto you.' As a woman, not just as your mother, I'm giving you these flowers as a lesson in what *every* woman you'll ever meet will enjoy receiving from you."

Use flowers as a way of cultivating in your child an appreciation for beauty. Point out beautiful gardens to your child as you drive through the neighborhoods of your city. Point out beautiful flowers as you take a walk with your child. That way your gift of flowers will not only be a love gift, but a gift of beauty.

- Surprise your child with flowers.
  Robert didn't expect to come home from school to find a big bouquet of roses in his very, very messy room. The note on them said, "I love you —even if I can't stand to be in your room."

  Robert's mother came home from work late that evening to find, as she peeked into her son's room to say goodnight, a much cleaner room. And in her own room she found one of the roses with a note to her: "I love you, too, Mom!"

  Shari didn't expect flowers as she finished her first piano lesson. "Concert pianists usually get flowers after they've finished a performance," her mother explained. "I don't expect you to be a concert pianist, but I do hope you'll always enjoy your own performances at the piano."
- Give flowers to your child on the same occasions in which you would consider giving flowers to an adult.
  After his dog died, Troy found a garden bouquet in his room. The note said simply, "I'm sorry. Love, Mom."

  When Lisa turned sixteen, she received a bouquet of a dozen pink roses, delivered to her at school. "Happy birthday, sweetheart. Love, Dad and Mother."
- Give your child a plant or tree or bush that can

then be transplanted into your garden. Let your child help with the transplanting. Andy received a tree as a gift the day after he had finally reached the four-foot mark on the height chart posted on the back of his bedroom door. "You're really growing up, son. Let's help something else grow up, too. Love, Dad." Father and son planted the tree together and both parents noted that Andy frequently referred to it as his tree. Nearly twenty years later Andy told his six-year-old daughter during a visit to Grandma's and Grandpa's house, "See that tree? That's my four-foot tree. When you hit four feet, we're going to plant a tree together in *our* yard!"

In our family we had azalea row. I can walk alongside it and say, "There's the one that Mom got from Dad when I was born . . . and that's the one that I gave Mom for her fiftieth birthday . . . and this is the one that we received when Grandpa died." That azalea bed is more than beautiful; it's history.

Flowers help underscore certain events for your child. They make certain moments more memorable. Flowers give your child a tangible, visual example of your love. Share them generously.

# 18 ✦ Be Willing to Let Go

Two of the greatest things any parent can ever give a child are a firm foundation of love and wings.

- Encourage your child to explore his world. As a parent, you have the prerogative to set boundaries and limits for your child, but within those boundaries, allow your child to explore freely.

  The boundary may be the backyard fence. The boundary lines may be "from the bench to the tree to the sandbox" at the park. The boundary may be "our block."
- Provide adventure books for your child, especially biographies of explorers, missionaries, travelers, adventurers. Give wings to your child's imagination. Let your child know, *"There's nobody I'd rather share the world with than you. I want you to have the freedom to pursue your interests and to fully explore your world."*
- Encourage your child to have relationships with children her age as well as with other caring adults. Give your child "permission" to love others and to create memories that don't include you.
- Encourage your child to explore his own poten-

tial and to take risks of creativity, effort, and of giving.

Alice had wanted to take skiing lessons for as long as anyone could remember. Alice's mother was frightened to let her daughter out on the slopes, since she herself had broken her leg as a child while learning to ski. Alice did just fine.

When Paul asked if he could try out for the boy's choir, his parents were astonished. They had never heard him sing. In fact, they had been told by a kindergarten teacher that Paul was tone deaf. "Are you sure?" asked Mother. "Yes," said Paul. "It's something I want to try." He did. He made the choir. He was even given a solo part at a concert.

One of your main responsibilities as an adult is to prepare your child to leave home one day. Incorporate statements such as these into your conversations:

- "When you visit that nation some day . . ."
- "I can hardly wait to see how you'll decorate your own apartment someday . . ."
- "In case you have to travel someday in your business or your job . . ."

Use these phrases as you teach your child important skills, from cooking to repairing to ordering food to packing to sewing.

When your child rebels against a rule you have

established or questions your abilities as a parent, you can always say:

- "Someday when you are an adult and out on your own, you may choose to . . ."

Children's security is not rooted in their being tied to your apron strings; it is in knowing that they have the freedom to be with you and the freedom to be on their own.

"One of the sounds that I miss most since Joe left for college is the sound of the screen door slamming," said his mother Gladys. "Very early on, Ed and I decided that we would put a low latch on the screen door so that Joe could always come and go from the house as he wanted. That way we weren't interrupted, and he wasn't inhibited. He must have gone in and out of the house a hundred times a day. We did require, of course, that he kill every fly that he let in! We felt it was important that Joe know that we were always here when he needed us, but that at the same time, we expected him to go out and make a mark on the world."

It is your job as a parent to train up your child to assume an adult role in our society. Wean your child. Encourage his growth and independence. Letting go is one of the most loving things you will ever do for your child.

# 19 ✦ A Note of Surprise

Tuck a little surprise message into a corner of your child's life. Say "I love you" in a moment when your child least expects it.

It might be a note glued to the bottom of the lunchbox: *"Hi. I ♥ you!"*

It might be a note tucked into a sock in the suitcase that goes off to camp. *"I love you!"*

It might be a message on a sheet of paper in your child's binder. *"I'm praying for you today!"*

It might be a photo of a big fish that your child discovers in his tackle box as he goes on his first overnight fishing trip. *"I'm wishing you lots of luck!"*

Joanne recently told me about a habit her mother has had for the past twenty-five years. Her mother removes the stickers on fruit—bananas, melons, and the like—and immediately puts them someplace in her children's rooms, on their clothes, or among their possessions. All their growing up years, Joanne and her two brothers have found "Ripe" and "Chiquita Banana" stickers on the pages of their schoolbooks, on bedroom mirrors, on the labels of a favorite T-shirt or blouse, folded inside a washcloth in the bathroom, just about anyplace that's unexpected. The message conveyed was and is a simple one, "I'm thinking of you. I'm loving you even from afar."

Recently Joanne's brother phoned her from Central America to say, "You'll never guess what I found stuck on a packet of underwear as I was unpacking my suitcase after a visit to Mom's. That's right . . . a fruit sticker that said, 'Fresh!' "

**Words of Encouragement**    To a child, words of encouragement are synonymous with "I love you"—

> *"Way to go!"*
> *"I'm proud of you."*
> *"I believe in you."*
> *"I just know you can do it."*

Find a creative place to put that message. Choose a place where you are nearly one hundred percent sure your child will find it but will also be surprised to discover it. All of these phrases say to a child, "Mom and Dad believe in me. They love me enough to tell me so."

To a child, these are also messages that are readily understood as complimentary ways of saying, "Mom and Dad are behind me. They believe in me. They love me enough to stand with me." To your child, a sincere compliment or a word of thanks is also perceived as a message of love.

Scott reached into his fielder's mitt one day to pull out a message, "Mitt of a champion." It put a smile on his face and a calm in his heart as he headed out into right field for the first inning of the championship game.

"An American hero . . . a true trooper." That was the note left beside a plate with a couple of chocolate chip cookies when Terisa came home from a full day of picking up roadside litter with her Girl Scout troop.

One father rented a billboard-type sign and had it placed in front of the family home. "Home of the world's greatest third grader."

Another parent used his daughter's sidewalk chalk to write a giant message to his daughter on the driveway of their home.

**Notes of Sincerity**  Your notes don't need to be elaborate or expensive. They don't need to be daily. They don't need to be messages that anyone will see other than your child. They only need to be sincere. You can write them on a paper bag holding a granola bar that is stuffed inside a backpack, a crumpled up wad of notebook paper that's stuffed into the sleeve of a jacket, or a piece of masking tape that is taped to a basketball.

Make your expressions of love a surprise. Your child will know, "Mom loves me even when I'm out of her sight. Dad cares even when I'm not aware of it."

# 20 ✦ "Snap Out of It" or "Get Beyond It" Can Be Messages of Love

You will face a number of times in the course of raising your child in which "Snap out of it!" or "Get beyond it!" can be the greatest expression of concern and love you can show your child.

"Snap out of it" is another way of saying, "I love you too much to let you grow up to be a miserable person." You need to be on the alert for two types of behavior that can result in misery for your child down the line: whining and whimpering.

**Whining**   A whining child is a miserable child to be around. Many adults overlook the fact that a child whines because he, too, is miserable.

What causes whining? Generally speaking, whining is caused by an unfulfilled expectation on the part of the child. The child wants something that he isn't being given. It may be attention, a toy, a second piece of candy, favor or acknowledgement from an adult, permission, a reward of some type—all of which boil down to the child's wish or will not being fulfilled or recognized.

Tell your child simply but firmly, "I refuse to allow you to grow up to be a miserable person. I will not accept whining. Not only will you not get what you want, but you will be sent to your room. I won't listen to this mournful sound. I want to see a happy face and, more importantly, a happy attitude. You can choose to be happy or content in this situation. You can choose to accept what you have and be grateful for it. You can choose to accept no for an answer."

If your child continues to whine, follow through. Send the child to his room or away from the rest of the group. Isolation stops whining faster than just about any other punishment. Go to your child later. If the whining starts again, leave your child alone or send him to his room a second time. In fact, leave your child alone until you get a positive answer to your question, "Are you ready to rejoin us with a happy heart?"

**Whimpering** There are many times when a child is truly hurt and she cries. She may have made a mistake or embarrassed herself in some way or been rejected or have experienced a bout of fear grounded in either an imaginary or real cause. Crying is an appropriate response for a child at such times, and the appropriate response from a parent is to hold the child and comfort her.

There are other times when a child whimpers because she simply isn't getting her way. She doesn't want to be left alone with the babysitter. She doesn't want to walk into her new classroom. She doesn't want big brother to reclaim his truck. Such cries are rooted in manipulation and ring false. Nearly every parent can tell in a second a real cry from a fake one.

Life holds many small challenges for a child, many unknowns and many risks. But a child will have the courage to face these challenges if he knows, "Mom thinks I can do this." Don't add to your child's doubts by displaying behavior that convinces your child he cannot handle the situation: "You're scared, so I'll stay."

Let your child know that life has tough moments but that you believe he can survive them. *"I know this may seem scary or hard for you to do, but I also know that you can do it. You have what it takes to make the most out of this hour without me. You have what it takes to turn a tough time into a terrific time."*

Love your child enough to insist that your child have a bright, positive attitude. "But that just isn't the personality of my child," you may say.

One of the most repeated phrases in the Bible is this: "Fear not. Rejoice!" Those words are stated as commands. Fear is not an acceptable behavior; joy is required. You have the privilege as a parent to say to your child, "Rejoice. And again I say, rejoice."

e you so much
that I want to give you this ..... at I treasure."
What makes an item an heirloom? The fact that you
like it and count it as a special item, or the fact that
you have made it and, thus, it represents your time,
effort, and skill.

### *What to Give*    The item may be . . .

- a family photo album.
- a quilt.
- a painting.
- a family Bible.
- a rare book.
- a coin or stamp collection.
- a piece of furniture.
- a musical instrument.
- a watch.
- anything you value highly.

Such gifts convey to a child, "I'm glad you're part
of this family. As a treasured child, you are worthy of
family treasures."

**When to Give It**    When should you give heirloom items to a child? When you are willing to let go of them and never ask about them again.

In many cases, especially with items easily broken or lost, you may want to let your child know, "This is going to be yours someday. It's my desire that you have it and that you will appreciate it so much that you will want to pass it along to someone you love as much as I love you." Mark the item with your child's name.

In some cases, you may want to keep an item on a high shelf or in a glass case for protection until such time as your child is old enough to take proper care of it. But once you have given an item you consider to be an heirloom to a child, don't ask about it, look for it, or even think about it. Consider it "passed along" and no longer yours. There's always a chance that your child won't value the item as much as you do. Don't let disappointment or resentment creep in. If you suspect that you are going to be hurt if the item is damaged, lost, or ignored, hold on to it until a later time or make it part of the estate you leave your child.

Giving heirloom items to your child sends two messages to your child. "I love you enough to give you this treasured item. And I expect you to live long, to prosper, and to extend the quality and character of our family to another generation. Toward that end, I give you a family treasure." Both of those messages are laden with love.

# 22 ✦ Introduce Your Child

Don't let your child be invisible. Introduce him. Acknowledge her. Include your child wherever you are and with whomever you come into contact.

The child who is not introduced is a child who can easily conclude, "Dad's ashamed of me. Mom's forgotten me. I'm not worth much. They must love the attention of that person more than they value my feelings." It's not a very great leap for your child to feel unwanted and unloved.

***Include Your Child***   Your child can learn something about you by being included in your conversations with other adults. He can discover that you are a valued member of another group, a work force or a club or a church group. He can discover that in your past, you were a lot like him.

If you need to discuss something privately with an adult you encounter, ask your child's permission for a few minutes alone with the person. "Sweetheart, I'm sure all this military talk is boring to you. If you'd like to go check out the Zingo ride, I'll meet you there in just a few minutes." Or, "Son, I need just a few seconds with Mrs. Jefferson to ask her a couple of questions. Would you mind taking these packages to the car?"

When you host a party, don't banish your children to an out-of-the-way corner. Introduce them to various guests. Let them sample the food you are serving. Let them enjoy a little of the party atmosphere. Then you can send them to bed or encourage them to go outside and play.

### *Teach Your Child*    Teach your child:

- How to address adults. (Always give your child a clue. "This is Mrs. Jefferson." "This is Dr. Jones." Encourage your child to call adults by a title and last name.)
- How to shake hands. (Firmly.)
- How to handle compliments. (A simple thank you is generally sufficient.)
- How to interrupt graciously. ("Excuse me" instead of a tug on the sleeve.)

Including your child in adult conversations does two things for your child. First, it says to your child that you consider him worthy to be included and that you value his presence.

Second, it trains your child in important communication skills. It says to your child, "I want you always to be able to talk with anyone, anywhere. I want them to remember you when they meet you. You're worth remembering." A child who is included feels loved.

# 23 ✦ Have a Listening Ear

Listen to your child. It may sound overly simplistic, but the axiom is generally true: *listen to your child, and chances are, he'll listen to you.*

**Clear Your Schedule**   Establish a time in your daily routine in which your child always knows that he can talk to you, whether he chooses to exercise that option or not. It may be while you are fixing dinner or in the quiet evening hours as you settle in for the night. It may be as soon as your child arrives home from school or in the car on the way to school.

Set apart time for being with your child. Make your time available to your child. (Make certain your child's calls can always get past a secretary or receptionist and through to you.)

**Clear Your Mind**   *Clear your mind* so that you can truly "hear" what your child is telling you. Very often, the first thing that a child says to you is not what he ultimately wants to share with you. Learn to ask questions of your child without interrogating him. Ask, "How'd algebra go today?" instead of "Did you pass?"

Ask your child questions that can't be answered

with a simple yes or no. Ask, "What was the best thing that happened at school today?" instead of, "Did you have a good day at school?"

Help your child switch gears from his day's work. Help him unwind. Ask, "Hear any good jokes today?" instead of "How much homework do you have to do?"

Go into a listening time with a positive frame of mind. "I definitely sense something is about to be added to the prayer list. Care to share it?"

***Clear Away the Clutter***   Turn off competing noises and chatter. Turn off the television set or the car radio. A segue may be helpful in establishing a listening mood.

- Provide an afternoon snack and sit down with your child to enjoy it with him.
- Read with your child for a few minutes. That's often a time when your child will be willing to exchange a few more words with you.
- Sit on the edge of the bed with your child for a few minutes after—or before—bedtime prayers.

A child who knows you have a listening ear is a child who knows you have a loving heart.

# 24 ✦ Send a Card

Give your child the excitement and fun of receiving a card in the mailbox addressed just to him! Have you ever noticed that adults seem to get all the mail? From a child's perspective, "getting mail" is an adult activity, including sorting the mail, opening it, and discarding it. When a child receives a piece of mail all his own, addressed specifically to him at his own home, he not only receives a wonderful treat, but as part of the very process, an important threefold message.

- You are an important part of this world, as important as any adult. Adult systems can also be enjoyed and employed by children. A part of growing up is learning how and when to use these systems.
- You have a place at this address, in this home.
- You have total control over the mail you receive. It is your privilege to open it, keep it or throw it away, read it or not, and respond or not.

Cards are a graphic way of underscoring what you say to your child orally. Children can hold a card. By touching it and "possessing" it, they experience its message in a way that is different from hearing the spoken word. Children can reread a card . . . and reread it. Children are concrete thinkers. They often believe a written message more than a verbal one simply because it is something they can see and touch.

Young children will often carry their cards until they are tattered and well splattered. "Mine," they say. My card, my mom and dad (or aunt, uncle, grandparent, godparent, or other friend)—my loving relationship.

Cards are also a great way for parents who travel a great deal to send a message of love to their children.

Rene's father is a truck driver. He sends her cards that she sometimes receives even after her father has returned home from a run. They are important to her, nevertheless, as an expression that even though her father is away a great deal of the time, he carries her in his heart.

Remember your children, too, as you send greeting cards at traditional times. Eight-year-old Kay Ellen has a scrapbook with nothing but birthday cards and birthday party photos in it. She has cards for each birthday from her aunt, both sets of her grandparents, and her parents, even cards for her first two birthdays, which she doesn't remember.

Cards are a good way for you to communicate with a child who is away at camp or visiting a relative. Try sending a humorous card. Will's mother did, with an added note, "I thought you might need a laugh about now." Little did she know that the card would arrive the same day that her son broke out with poison ivy welts.

Finally, cards are a way for your child to show others that you care. They are subtle but important evidence: "My Mommy sent me this. My Mommy loves me." Feeling your love is critically important to your child. It is also important for your child to be able to declare the fact of your love to others.

You should also feel free to make your own cards. Have a cut and paste session with your child periodically. Let her cut the illustrations from cards that have previously been sent to you and turn them into new cards. Then, turn right around and send one of those cards to your child with a message of love and appreciation. "Thanks, honey, for helping us save a tree." Or, "I couldn't have done it without you!"

- Cards are inexpensive.
- They take relatively little time to choose and send.
- They offer you a "platform" of thoughts to which you may add other lines that you find difficult to say in a face-to-face encounter.

All in all, cards are a great way to say "I love you" to a child.

# 25 ✦ Project the Fact of Your Love into the Future

Share a vision with your child for what you hope your child's life will be like in the future, even for all eternity. Include your love and a loving relationship with your child as part of that vision. Let your child know that you expect your love for him to last forever.

This does *not* mean that you should tell your child what you expect him to do in his future or what he should choose as a career. Insist that your child prepare for his future by acquiring certain skills, from learning to make his own bed to staying in school). But mostly, take delight in your child as she discovers her own potential and makes decisions about her own career path.

What you *can* say to your child are statements such as these:

- *"I can hardly wait to see what our lives are like fifty years from now. You'll probably be telling me to buckle my seatbelt on the way to the grocery store, just as I am telling you now. What kind of car do you suppose we'll be riding in?"*
- *"I look forward to the day when you'll invite me to your house for dinner. I hope we can laugh and*

> *have a good time in your kitchen, just like we do
> now. I wonder what you'll fix? What do you think,
> hot dogs or hamburgers?"*

- *"I'm going to miss you when you go off to college.
  Life will have fewer surprises, such as discovering
  what is stuffed under your bed. Life will also be a
  lot quieter. I'm not sure I'll be able to handle the
  opportunity to use the phone whenever I want! It's
  going to be fun, though, to see what major you
  choose."*

Weave your projections of a future loving relationship into the casual course of daily life. Let your child begin to imagine the close parent-child relationship you will have in the future. Let him know that you expect to be a part of his life always as a loving supportive person.

This does *not* mean you should convey that you expect to live with your child or that you have a desire for your child always to be dependent upon you. Quite the contrary. Establish an expectation that your child will one day be an independent adult and that you look forward to communicating and relating to him as such. Establish an expectation that although the nature of your relationship may change, the love between you will never be diminished.

- After a conversation with your child on a serious topic or a conversation in which you have shared hard-to-express emotions, you may want to say in conclusion, "I hope we can always have good conversations like this. I hope you always feel that you can talk to me."

• After a joking, playful, fun time, let your child know, "I can't imagine not being able to laugh with you for the next hundred thousand million years!"

• After a time of punishment, hug your child and assure him, "You know something? Someday you're going to be too big for me to spank, but you're never going to be too big for me to hug!"

Let your child know, too, that you believe in his ability to be a moral, law-abiding citizen. Letting your child know that you believe in his bright side, his ability to do good, and in his opportunities for success is another way of saying, "I love you and from the vantage point of my love, I can see wonderful attributes within you."

Love means hoping for your child's best success, believing in your child's best nature, and looking forward to your child's best gifts to the world. Share this loving vision with your child. It is a way of conveying, "My love for you will never end."

# 26 ✦ Encourage and Establish Private Jokes

Share enough experiences with your child and you will end up with a bucketful of private jokes—fun, playful, just-you-two memories that your child will cherish all his life. Your child will know that "Dad and I have a good time when we're together. Mom and I laugh a lot. We're on the same wavelength. Our hearts are beating in tune."

My grandfather had a wonderful ability to distill his love into a wink (accompanied by just the hint of a smile). No matter what Grandma was saying or Mom was doing, no matter where we were or what the circumstances, Grandpa could send a large dose of love straight from his heart to mine in a fleeting instant. I was always surprised when he turned to me and winked. I was always pleased.

What makes for a private joke? A moment of teasing that you both enjoy, a shared sense of what is humorous in the world, an ability to laugh at the human condition.

Teasing isn't fun if the one being teased doesn't think so. Then teasing is perceived as harrassment. (Siblings know this far more readily than parents sometimes.)

**Some Guidelines**   Be sure you observe some simple guidelines for teasing:

- Tease your child only if you are willing to be teased back.
- Even as you tease, respect your child. Don't tease about his mistakes, his accomplishments, or about any behavior that you or your child are trying to change (or which you think should be changed). In other words, don't tease a child about anything over which he is perceived to have some degree of control. Tease him about the funny tie he chooses to wear but not about his weight or his stammering.
- Never tease a child in front of his friends or strangers.
- Tease primarily in the context of imaginary situations. ("We're in big trouble if we ever take Gabbie to the zoo. Imagine an elephant coming over to greet him the way his dog just did!")
- Tease always with love, never as a method of teaching or as a punishment.

**Encourage Laughter**   Let your child know that laughter is a wonderful commodity in our world. Laugh aloud at the movie you attend with your child. Laugh aloud at the circus clown. Laugh aloud at cartoons you watch with your child.

I've never met a young child who didn't find a certain amount of humor in physical comedy, the pie-in-the-face slapstick variety. Adults often try to stifle their amusement at those types of comedic situations because they don't want to encourage such behavior in their children. Go ahead and laugh! Let your child know it's OK to laugh at performers who are doing a show in which slapstick humor is included. Point out that the people in the show aren't really injured but that it is *never* appropriate to laugh at someone who truly is injured or sick.

Never laugh at your child. Teach him to laugh at himself. How? By laughing at your own self!

Make light of what might seem like embarrassing moments. Don't overemphasize them, ignore them, or be chagrined by them.

If you can laugh at yourself, and your child sees that you can, your child will learn to laugh at himself. He will find pleasure in human differences and in the little accidents of life.

Laughing with your child in this manner conveys an important message to your child: "My love is not contingent on your perfection. You are a human being. So am I. The love between us transcends our human foibles."

# 27 ✦ Apologize When You Need To

Let your child know that you make mistakes, that you aren't the perfect parent. Admit your mistakes. Confess them. Let your child know you will most likely make mistakes in the future, even though you don't want to make them.

***Admit Your Mistakes*** Perfection is a terrible burden for both you and your child. I have yet to meet a child who didn't forgive and who didn't respond with love to a parent who admitted a mistake. That's good news! Accepted apologies bring healing to your child and to your relationship. Hearing and accepting your apologies allows your child to let go of feelings of resentment before they can fester into bitterness.

By admitting your own mistakes and letting your child hear that your love transcends your mistakes, you are also giving your child the confidence that comes through knowing that no mistake, error, goof, flub, or accident that *he* commits can destroy the love you feel for him.

Establish again and again that your love is not based on perfect behavior, either yours or your child's. Love transcends behavior.

I've never believed the line from the movie *Love Story* in which the heroine says to her beloved, "Love means never having to say you're sorry." In my opinion, love means that you are *always* willing to say you're sorry when you have done something that has caused hurt to another person.

**Pick the Right Time**   When should you apologize?

- In a private moment. Don't grandstand; your child will find your apology to be insincere. You may need to apologize publicly if the mistake you have made is a public one that included people other than your child. In those cases, apologize to your child first. Let him know that you are *most* sorry that he was hurt by your behavior.
- Never apologize unless you are truly sorry for the thing you have done. Some people apologize solely to smooth over a tense situation or to appease someone else, while, in their heart of hearts, they aren't the least bit repentant.
- Only apologize to the extent that you feel regret. You may have *no* regret for punishing your child for his knocking over the entire cookie display in a willful act of anger-filled disobedience at the supermarket. You may, however, be sorry that you spanked your child right there in the supermarket aisle. Apologize, in that case, for

the way in which you punished your child, not for the fact that you did.

- If your child was hurt as the result of an accident on your part, apologize for the fact of the accident. Assure your child that it was an accident, not a willful act on your part. (Your child probably already knows this, but it doesn't hurt for you to say so.) Don't self-justify. Apologize for being the source of pain.

- Don't bother with an apology if you have no intention of changing your future behavior so as *not* to make the same mistake again. It is a hollow apology to say, "I'm sorry I hit you last night" as a consequence of having had too much alcohol—unless you stop drinking (and seek the help that may be necessary to enable you to stop).

- Don't try to cover up your own bad behavior with an apology. Don't assume that just because you apologize each time you are late picking your daughter up at her dance class that you can continue to be late. Your child will eventually know that your apology is just so many empty words.

Your apologies, in sum, must be genuine, heartfelt, and bear the fruit of changed behavior. If they don't, they will be perceived by your child as lies. How, then, can your child trust you when you say "I love you?"

# 28 ✦ Have a Special Whistle Just for Your Child

I can't duplicate the whistle that my father has used to get my attention ever since I was born. I just can't seem to make the sound he does, even though I have tried repeatedly.

Recently my father and I became separated as we were shopping in a large department store. I continued to browse through the racks of clothing, unaware that he had gone in another direction and had lost sight of me. Suddenly, I heard that familiar "daddy call." I found him in a matter of seconds, much to the surprise of the clerk standing next to him.

"But," she sputtered, "how did you hear him? Nobody else paid any attention."

"I come when he calls," I said with a laugh. "Just like a well-conditioned puppy!"

***A Reward*** Although I was attempting to be humorous, in actuality, Daddy's whistle *has* had some conditioning associated with it. I have always been rewarded for responding by being in my father's presence. His whistle is associated with being safe, protected, found, related, loved.

Ultimately, the message has always been the same. "Daddy loves me enough to find me. He wants my attention. He wants me to be with him. He wants me to see him or hear him."

**A Warning**    I am fairly certain my brother has a little different feeling about Daddy's whistle. He has generally heard it at times when he was doing something that he shouldn't have been doing. To him, the whistle is a call to "get out of the trouble you're about to get yourself into."

**A Call to Attention**    I was surprised one day to hear my friend Ellie call her children. She used a different whistle, one unique to her family. "It comes in handy," she said, "when you have two explorers for children. They follow their noses faster than my feet can move." What does Ellie's whistle convey to her children? The same message: "Mommy loves us enough to find us. She wants us to be with her."

A love whistle gives your child confidence that "Daddy knows how to get in touch with me if we lose touch. He loves me and doesn't want to lose me. Mommy cares enough about me to get my attention when I'm about to make a mistake. She loves me and doesn't want me to get in trouble."

# 29 ✦ Take Time to Play with Your Child

Have a playtime with your child every day. Let your child know that you like his world, and that you want to have fun with him doing the things that he likes to do.

A few years ago, I encountered a boy named Bert. Bert was a real brat, always creating trouble, always looking for a way out of trouble, always justifying the trouble he caused.

Something wonderful happened to Bert, however. His father put down his newspaper and turned off the TV and started playing games with his son. Dad spotted a real ability in Bert to think ahead and to manipulate. He channeled that ability into a few chess lessons.

In themselves, the chess games didn't generate a lot of conversation, but they did create a bond. Bert felt less and less need to get his father's attention.

Dad also applied some of the rules of chess to other areas of life. ("The Queen is the player that is the most valuable because she can move in all directions. Life's like that. You want to be able to move in all directions. You need an education to do that.") Bert listened.

***Learning Through Play***    Bert learned to play by the rules, in life as well as the game of chess. He learned how to call on the advice and help of others. He learned how to compete; how to win and lose. The truths encountered in the example of Bert and his father can be applied to nearly all game-playing activity between parents and their children.

- Through playtime, your child acquires an ever-growing awareness that you are available to him.
- Through playtime, your child learns how to play.
- Through playtime, your child finds a relaxed environment for communicating with you.
- Through playtime, your child learns that skills can be improved.
- Through playtime, your child learns how *you* play.

***Who Makes the Rules?***    Within the bounds of safety and morality, let your child set the rules and limits. *"You take the white piece, I'll take the red one."* Let your child dictate the pace of the play and govern the match.

If you must make suggestions, do so only to trigger imagination. Don't force your ideas.

Play with your child. He will have your time. He will have your attention. He will have numerous opportunities for learning, growing, sharing. In that, he will feel your love.

# 30 ✦ Give Equal Attention to Each Child

One of the Smothers Brothers' famous comedy routines is based on the principle, "Mom loved you best." We laugh, in part, because we recognize or have experienced the truth underlying the jest.

**Be Fair to Each Child**   Did you take eighteen hours of videotape of your firstborn, only to forget to pull out the camcorder once your second or third child arrived? Do you have an album full of photos of your firstborn and only a smattering of snapshots of your other children?

Does your daughter have claim to all the family linens, quilts, and other heirloom needlepoint? What about your son?

Are you making plans to help your son buy a car when he turns sixteen? Do you talk about helping your daughter in the same way?

- Your child needs to know that he or she has *equal access to your time and attention.* Each child needs to know, "Mom has time just for *me.*" This is especially true when a new baby arrives in a family and the older child or children tend to get lost in the shuffle.

- Your child needs *equal access to your applause.* Each child needs to be able to count on her parents to be present for her performances, with loud applause and the heart of a fan.
- Your child needs *equal access to your display of pride.* The disparaging difference in photo albums is an example of unequal display of pride. In this instance, the problem could be remedied simply by sitting down at the beginning of each new year and scheduling two or three "photo shoot" days on your family calendar.
- Your child needs *equal access to your gifts.* Older children and favored children tend to get more of "the good stuff." Money flows more freely when there is one child instead of five.
- Your child needs *equal access to an inheritance.* No matter the reasons that may be cited, no child ever understands an unequal dividing of family property or heirloom treasures.

***Each Child Is Unique***    Each child's personality is different. Sometimes you will find that you understand one child better than another or that you empathize with one child more than another or that your personality meshes better with one child more than another. Those differences are normal and to be expected. Your child probably enjoys being with one parent more than the other in certain circumstances.

Don't let these differences, however, influence your love. You do have enough love for each child.

# 31 ✦ Take Your Child with You

Just as you find time to play with your child, give your child an opportunity to enter into your world. This, too, conveys the message, "I love you and enjoy being with you!"

In early November, my father often allowed me to ride with him during his evening trips to take loaded cotton trailers to the gin. I still remember those times of togetherness, of braving the dark unknown, accomplishing an important task, and greeting the gin clerks as if I were a "big girl." It seemed special to be allowed to go out at night; it must have been all of 6:30 P.M.!

**In the Workplace** John takes his children to the office on Saturday mornings when he goes in to catch up on the week's mail. The children sit in the conference room adjacent to his office and have a task of their own to complete during the hour or two they are in the office: a set of new crayola pictures for the bulletin board that hangs on the back of John's door.

Occasionally John will call his children on the phone that connects the two rooms, just to see if there is anything they need. They know their way down to the office cafeteria, and at least once during the morning, they all head for the coffee and hot chocolate vending machines. Mostly, they work, and he works.

John's children have a good idea where Daddy is when he isn't at home, what their Daddy does during the day, and how their daddy feels about work. At the end of their mutual work session, the children hang up their drawings, and they all make the rounds through the office in order that John might leave messages on various desks and check to make certain that various machines have been left on or turned off.

**Running Errands**    Andrea takes her daughters with her every time she goes to the beauty shop to have her hair cut, frosted, or permed. Sometimes her two daughters have their hair cut. Most of the time, they sit and read the books they have brought along, watch the various procedures, and choose styles from books provided by the shop. Once, Andrea treated them to a manicure.

Over the years, the girls have learned a lot by watching people come and go. They have learned that everybody likes a different style, that it takes organizational ability to do just about any task in life, and that it is important to be able to communicate exactly how short you want your bangs cut! They are experiencing a part of their mother's world. They know that Mom enjoys their company and wants them to share her life.

# 32 ✦ Honor Your Child's Privacy

Don't snoop through his things. Don't read her diary. Don't monitor his phone calls. Don't rummage through her special box of treasures.

Honor your child's right to privacy. That sends a message to your child: "I love you enough to trust you. There's nothing you can do or hide that will destroy my love for you. At the same time, I don't need to know everything you say or do. My love is not rooted in your behavior, but in who you are as my child. I love you enough to let you become independent, but I also love you enough to insist that you never become alienated."

Very often, family arguments over privacy stem from a lack of initial, clear definitions as to what may be considered private and what may not be.

**A Parent's Requirements**  Your child's room is not only your *child's* room. It is a room in *your* house. You can require that it be kept clean (with neatness negotiable), that no structural damage be done (such as a hole in the wall), and no structural changes be made without your permission (including curtains pulled from their rods), that certain limitations may be placed on decor (no nude posters, perhaps), and that certain items may not be kept in it (snakes, for example).

Let your child know that you plan to clean his room periodically. (The alternative, of course, is for your child to do the cleaning and to do a thorough job of it.)

Tell your child you retain the right to enter her room any time you smell smoke. Let your child know that if she has friends over and chooses to entertain them in her room, that you consider her room to have then taken on the nature of a public meeting place and that you retain the right to enter at any time, although you will knock first and not stay. You may require that the door be left open if your teenager entertains someone of the opposite sex.

**A Child's Privilege**    You can—and should— designate certain areas within your child's room as "private." Your child's diary is private. So is a box for keeping letters. The top drawer of your child's desk may be a place for private things. You may even want to give your child a box, desk, or locker space that can be locked. (Make sure you have a spare key somewhere so you can gain access should your child lose his key.) Your child's conversations with his friends are private.

However, you have the privilege of determining what is allowed inside your home. That includes what books and magazines may be kept in your home, what programs may be watched or listened to (in your child's room, too, not only on the main set downstairs), what music is aired, what games can be played, and who and what may be allowed access into your home (four-legged, two-legged, and no-legged creatures!)

By establishing the limits of your child's privacy, you are also extending the freedoms of it. Your child can have the assurance that his phone calls will not be monitored, that his correspondence will not be censored, that his conversations and activities with his friends will not be spied upon, and above all, that you desire for him to be a responsible person who will make responsible choices.

You may make errors in setting the boundaries of privacy or in allowing certain items into your home. You must never err, however, in retaining the right to determine the limits of privacy.

You are also conveying three of the most important "tough love" lessons your child needs to learn under your roof:

- Love is a means for getting along in a society— in a family, in a community, in a group. It is not a license for doing anything you want to do or for alienating yourself from a group norm.
- Love does not free us to do evil. Love constrains us from doing evil.
- Love is the motive for extending, sharing, and promoting life—not limiting it, harming it, or destroying it.

# 33 ✦ Have a "Date" with Your Child

Make being with your child an active choice, not a consequence: "I'll be with my child if there's nothing else to do." Choose to be with your child.

Let your child hear you say to someone that he knows you enjoy being with: "Oh, I'd like to go with you, but I have a prior date with my child."

***Plan a Date with Your Child.*** Spend an entire evening with your child. Choose to do it and count it as important, as important as you considered your first date with your spouse.

On your date, talk about what your child wants to talk about. That may mean a conversation devoted totally to the antics of the hottest TV character, the latest fad, or the current second-grader jokes. Eat what your child likes to eat. Go to his or her favorite restaurant. Be prepared for burgers or pizza.

From the time Melody was ten until she was eighteen, she had a date with her father on the second Friday night of every month ending in a *y* or an *r*—January, February, May, July, September, October, November, December.

Your date with your child need not be elaborate or

expensive. It need only be a date that you set, keep, and enjoy.

## Make an Appointment with Your Child.

Put it on your work calendar. Two o'clock on the first Thursday afternoon of the month. That was the set appointment time that Stell had with her daughter, Gracie. Stell gave Gracie a note to give to her teacher on Monday of the designated week and a second reminder note on Thursday morning.

Stell cleared her work schedule, allowing nothing to interfere. She had the "Thursday time" preestablished with her boss as a condition of her employment and worked through the lunch hour on Monday, Tuesday, and Wednesday of the first week of the month. On Thursdays, she left her office promptly at 1:30 P.M. and took a cab to pick up Gracie.

Once they were both in the cab, Stell and Gracie would change gears. Down came Stell's hair and off came her jewelry. She would pull casual shoes from her briefcase to replace her heels. They would stop by their apartment just long enough to dump their things and get right back into the same cab to head for the zoo, the park, the amusement park, or a late matinee movie. Just the two of them. They would have dinner out, maybe just a deli sandwich.

Once a month during the school year. Nine appointments a year for five years running. A total of forty-five, three-hour "appointments." A lifetime of happy memories.

# 34 ✦ Display Your Child's Photograph

Put your child on display—at least in a photographic format. Let your child see, in a tangible way, that you are proud of him and desire for others to know that he or she is your child. Send a message to your child: "I'm glad to be associated with you in the eyes of the world."

- *Have a photo of your child at your place of work —if that is appropriate—*on a desk, credenza, bookshelf. That way, when your child comes to see you in your place of employment, he will have the message reinforced: "My mother is thinking about me even when she can't be at home with me."
- *Carry your child's photograph in your wallet or purse.* My own father's wallet is about three inches thick. Why? Because he still carries at least a dozen of his favorite photographs of my brother and me. Every child loves to rummage through a daddy's wallet or a mommy's purse. Let them find themselves in the process.
- *Take photographs of your child with you as you travel.* Let your child see you packing his or her

framed photograph into your suitcase. The message? "Daddy is taking me along in his heart."

- *Have photographs of your child on display in your own home.* Give visitors the opportunity to admire them and your child the opportunity to see himself in the context of his own home. Especially have photographs in areas that you consider your private space—boudoir, bedroom, home office.

Include photos that show your child in action. Don't limit yourself to school pictures. Include photos that show you with your child. Include photos that remind you of special moments shared with your child, moments in which your child is discovering the world, moments in which your child displays spontaneous joy.

When displaying family photos in a grouping, include photos of yourself and your spouse as a child, as well as photos of grandparents and other family members. Let your child see himself as a valuable and welcome part of the whole clan. Express to your child the message of continuity, "You are an important member of our family. We all love you, just as we have loved one another down through the years."

Consider having a formal portrait taken of your child at least once or twice during his growing-up years.

Photographs say to your child, "Any scene is better with you in it." And that's an expression of love!

# 35 ✦ Require the Truth

Do not accept lies from your child—ever. Insist upon honesty. Do not let a pattern develop in which your child believes, "Mom (or Dad) has a tolerance for lies." Such a belief leads a child to conclude that "it's possible Mom and Dad are lying when they tell me they love me."

Speak the truth to your child. Continually pull your child back to reality and to an accountability for the truth. Children have an inborn capacity for imagination and for fantasy. Much of the growing-up experience for a child is actually a ferreting out of fact from fiction. It is the parent's role to continually call a child back from fantasy to face the real world.

This does *not* mean that you should avoid any activities that promote your child's ability to imagine. On the contrary, the development of your child's imagination is an important aspect of developing his creativity and his expressive potential. It *does* mean that you refuse to let your child dwell perpetually in a fantasy world.

**Fact versus Fiction** Talk with your child about the reality of television programs. Ask, "What was real in that story and what wasn't?" Ask, "Do you think people like that really exist?" Ask, "Why wouldn't that be a likely story in real life?" Help your child distinguish between fiction and documentary.

***Little White Lies*** Some parents find "little white lies" acceptable, even cute. Don't be among them. The telling of any lie instills a belief in a child that lying is not only acceptable but sometimes it is preferable and, occasionally, even fun. Lying becomes, all too easily, a means for manipulation of others.

The number-one hearer of your child's lie is not you, it is your child. A child hears himself lie and, in some small way, accepts his own lie as being true. Lies and truth thus become confused. A child who falls into the habit of telling lies eventually doesn't know *how* to tell the truth—to himself or to others—and may not even recognize the truth.

Keep your child's feet planted firmly in reality and let him take an occasional break to escape into an imaginary world with imaginary friends, a world in which he, no doubt, will be the hero or the star. Don't let your child live in a fantasy world, taking only an occasional reality break for brushing his teeth or tying his shoelaces.

## Practice Telling Details

- Ask your child to tell about an incident that really happened. You might say, "Darling, you tell the story about seeing the lions at Safari Land."

Encourage details. *"How many lions were there? What did they do? What did they look like? What was said by those of us in the car?"*

- Ask your child to play journalist. Point out to your child the necessity for details, the importance of facts, the descriptive power of elaboration. *"What did he say? What did she say? When? How? Where? Who? What was the result? Why do you think this happened?"*
- Ask your child to tell you about a book she has finished. *"What was the plot? What were the characters like? Where was the story set?"*

Such activities give your child practice in speaking the truth, in developing rationales, and in prioritizing information.

Finally, a child who is allowed to lie and get away with it begins to develop an assumption that all people lie and get away with it.

Love is based on trust. It is also based on truth. When you say to your child, "I love you," you want your child to believe you and to *know* that you are telling him or her the rock-bottom, no-frills truth. Allowing a pattern of lies to develop in your child's life clouds the capacity of your child to hear the truth of your love.

# 36 ✦ Give Your Child a Party

Every child loves to be the center of attention, even the child who seems the most shy or reserved. Nothing puts a child on center stage more than a party in his or her honor. Give your child

- a birthday party,
- a reception after confirmation or first communion or baptism,
- a graduation party (from any grade or course of study you choose).

Or just invite your child's friends over for an afternoon or evening of fun—a swim party, barbecue, costume party, or a Valentine dance.

There's nothing in the rule book of life that says you can't give your child a surprise party on any day of the year. It doesn't need to be in commemoration of a birthday.

If it is not a surprise party, let your child be the host or hostess of the party. Rehearse with your child in advance how to be a host, greet people, mingle among the guests, serve refreshments, make introductions, and bid guests good-bye at the door.

**A Mother-Daughter Social**   Early one autumn, Stacey invited five of her daughter's friends to a no-gifts, fancy-dress tea party. The moms were included in the invitation. The mothers dressed up and so did their daughters. Tables were set with lace and china. Mums were cut from the garden.

Shelley, Stacey's daughter, greeted all her friends at the door with a single flower, which the little girls then put into a vase to make a centerpiece bouquet. She showed each of her friends her placecard at the table.

While the little girls sipped punch and ate cookies and petit fours, the mothers sipped tea and coffee, ate finger sandwiches and lemon tarts, and watched their daughters through the slats of the louvered doors that separated their tea party from the one their daughters were enjoying.

As the afternoon drew to a conclusion, Stacey took a portrait-style photo of each girl and her mother out in their garden. (A few weeks later, guess what Stacey gave to her friends as Christmas presents?) Shelley loved being a hostess. Today, nearly twenty years later, she has her own catering and party-planning business.

**Memories of Love**   A party gives your child a wonderful opportunity to be the center of attention, to receive the thanks, congratulations, or kind words of friends or relatives. A party gives your child a memory that will last a lifetime.

# 37 ✦ Lend Your Moral Support in Times of Crisis or Challenge

Every parent walks a fine line between mothering and smothering, between being a hand-holding daddy and a hands-off father. Your child needs your moral support in two types of circumstances: when he is experiencing something or someone for the first time, and when he is feeling more fear than faith.

Learn to recognize these times. Be sensitive to them, and be there for your child. He will always remember your presence and support as a living example of your love.

Be there with encouragement and support when your child

- Has his or her first haircut.
- Goes to the doctor or dentist.
- Enters a new school or a new grade.
- Meets a new babysitter.

- Has his first stage performance.
- Leaves for her first date.

Identify those occasions when your child is facing a new routine, learning a new skill, or meeting a new group of people. *Be* there at those critical times.

## Ways to Show Support

- Tell your child as much as you can about what to expect. Explain how to make friends, how to ask getting-acquainted questions, what the rules are. Give your child as much advance preparation as possible. If your child is facing a performance, give him an opportunity for a dress rehearsal at home.
- Go with your child. Don't drop your child off at curbside. Go into the classroom, through the backstage doors, into the examining room.
- Help your child break the ice. Point out the familiar. Explain the unfamiliar. Make a few introductions or ask a few names.
- Give your child a parting show of encouragement—a thumbs-up sign, a wave, a blown kiss, a shoulder hug, a wink. Don't embarrass your child by staying around too long. At the same time, don't allow your child to cling to you. Let your child go to his seat in the class or on the team bench. Wait for a conversation to begin or for the adult in charge to take over. Disappear quietly and discreetly.

• Let your child know before you leave when you will be back and where you will be in the interim. Leave a phone number if you're going to be somewhere other than home or work. Make sure your child knows when and where he is going to be with you again.

It is a real mark of maturity for a child to reach the place where he says about a first encounter, "It's OK, you don't need to go in with me." When that happens, be pleased! Smile and say, "OK!"

A child who is habitually left alone to face new challenges may grow up to be tough, but he is also likely to have a less tender heart. Don't let your child come to the conclusion, "Mom says she loves me, but she abandons me just when I need her the most. Dad says he loves me, but he's never there when I need the security of his presence."

Love means being available to your child when your child needs you. Say "I love you" with your very presence.

# 38 ✦ Allow Your Child to Choose a Treat

From time to time, let your child choose a treat for no reason other than she is your child. Reinforce the overriding fact of your love, "I love you just because you are my son, my daughter!"

***Occasional Surprises*** Kelley lets her children create a kid's menu occasionally. She allows each of her four children to choose one food for the evening meal. (It can't be a dessert.) One recent meal combined steamed rice with butter, hot dogs (and buns), deviled eggs, and clam chowder. Another meal combined fish sticks, ravioli, applesauce, and peanut butter and jelly sandwiches.

About once a month, Sue will say to her daughter, "Why don't you choose something from the cosmetic counter while I do the grocery shopping? Top limit of six dollars!" Kristine has a great time deciding among the lipsticks, nail polishes, and other makeup items. At other times, Sue will give her the option of choosing any magazine she wants from the fairly extensive selection available in the same store. Kristine is learning to make choices and is receiving treats at the same time.

Surprise your child with an unexpected treat. Here are some examples.

- *"Why don't you pick out a package of cookies for us?"*
- *"Here's five dollars. I'm going to stay in the car while you run into the bakery and pick out two of your favorite donuts. Bring me one you think I'd like, too."*
- *"Let's each get a new CD. I reserve the right to approve the lyrics, though."*
- *"Let's stop and get an ice cream cone. Choose any flavor you want—one scoop or two!"*
- *"Here's ten dollars to spend on anything you like at the amusement park. If the item costs more than that, you'll have to use your own allowance money. If you don't want to buy anything, that's fine, too."*
- *"Let's stop here at this store on our way out so you can pick out a new bow for your hair. You decide."*

**Reasonable Limits**    At other times, insist that your child not beg, whine, or ask repeatedly for treats. Assure your child that you will provide for his or her basic needs. Remind your child that he can always use his allowance money or earnings for some items. Let treats be at your initiative.

Insist that your child not go beyond the treat you

designate. Define the treat clearly and stick with your definition. Not two hair bows—one. Not fifteen dollars—ten dollars. Not an ice cream sundae—a cone, with a two-scoop maximum.

Don't link your treats with a behavior. Let your child pick out a package of cookies or an album independent of a victory or loss in his life. Let your child be surprised with a treat that is totally unrelated to his performance or accomplishments.

Suggest treats that your child might think are for a slightly "older kid." Let your eleven-year-old choose a lipstick, with the clear stipulation that she can't wear lipstick in public and that this is only for practice before the mirror in her room. Let your twelve-year-old son pick out an after-shave to be used only on those occasions when he is wearing a suit. Your child will be surprised at your level of confidence in him.

Let the treat be enjoyed primarily by your child. Give your child the first cookie out of the package, the first piece of pie. Treats say to your child, "Mom and Dad think I'm special just for who I am." That's love!

# 39 ✦ Share a Song with Your Child

Celebrate the relationship you have with your child in song. Many lovers have a song they refer to as "our song," usually a song that evokes memories of an important time together—a first date, a first dance together, an engagement night. You and your child have a loving relationship, too, and a song can help remind your child of happy moments spent with you.

- *"Your song" may be a tune that you hear together on a joyful occasion.* Perhaps it is one you hear on the radio as you make your way to a favorite picnic ground, a song that's playing on your stereo one night when a giggly mood hits and you enjoy a wild 'n' crazy time washing dishes, a song that gets stuck on a mall loudspeaker as you are in the final rush of Christmas shopping. "Your song" can be whatever song you remember as the song related to an enjoyable moment you have shared.
- *"Your song" may be a piece of music that is played frequently in your home.* Peter grew up in a home in which both parents had a deep love for classical music. The music of Johannes Brahms was frequently playing on his parent's

stereo. Today, nearly fifteen years later, those symphonies still evoke for Peter a remembrance of his parent's cozy living room and quiet evenings spent working jigsaw puzzles with his father as his mother sat nearby working on a needlepoint project.

For Dorena, the music was jazz. Her father loved to listen to the early albums, and he had a number of 78s that he played on the family hi-fi console. When Dorena is feeling a little homesick these days, she goes to the listening section of the library near her dormitory and plays "memories of home." Dad and Mom seem a little closer.

- *"Your song" may be a song that you make up especially for your child.* You don't need to be a composer or lyricist to come up with a song that you sing just for your child. Pick a tune that is familiar to you or make up a tune, and sing whatever words come to mind. Make it a love song. Keep it simple. Use your child's name as part of the lyrics.

I made up a song for three of my godchildren who are all in the same family. I let them know early on that this song was just for them and that I didn't sing it to anyone else. The words are exceedingly simple: "Who loves Kurtie? I love Kurtie. Who loves Kurtie? I'm the one who does!" The same song works equally well for sisters Katelyn and Kiersten. The phrase "I'm

the one who does" is accompanied by tickles.
You are welcome to use it with your child.

- *"Your song" may be a hymn.* It might be a rousing rendition of *"Onward Christian Soldiers"*
  that you sing together while you're fixing sack
  lunches or *"Amazing Grace"* sung together occasionally as a family bedtime song or *"My Faith
  Looks Up to Thee"* sung to your child in cozy
  times of comfort. Choose a hymn that both you
  and your child enjoy. Learn all the verses, and
  sing it with gusto.

Don't be surprised if you hear your child singing
"your song" to himself as he plays quietly or
prepares himself for facing a new challenge. That's
the value of having a mutually loved song—your
child can sing it to evoke memories of your strength,
courage, presence, and zest for living at any time and
in virtually any place without calling too much attention to himself. Let a song encapsulate your love.
Sing or play it often.

# 40 ✦ Be Willing to Share Your Child with Other Adults

Don't set yourself up to be the only source of love your child experiences. Your child may not recognize the difference now, but he will feel cheated later. Share your child with other adults who love him. Let him know the joy of being loved by all of his grandparents, aunts and uncles, godparents, and other adults with whom he may have a bond.

The love from other adults serves as a reinforcement of your love. Their words of love back up your expressions of love and give your words, "I love you," even greater meaning. Their love brings your child to the conclusion that he is, indeed, lovable— not just by a parent who is often perceived as "having" to love the child, but by others who don't "have" to.

Often, parents knowingly, and sometimes unknowingly, attempt to shield their child from others because they, themselves, have been hurt. This is especially true in the case of divorce or separation. As hurt as you may have been, strive to see the world through your child's eyes. Your child will feel punished by you if he is denied access to those he has grown to love.

**Valued Companions** How can you tell which adults your child should have as regular companions? Let him be around those adults who value his presence and who enjoy being with him. Don't force your child on an unwilling grandparent. At the same time, recognize that you have the prerogative as a parent to define the rules of the relationship.

If no adult to whom your child is related lives within easy driving distance or if your child's grandparents and aunts and uncles are deceased, strive to find an adult with whom your child can spend time. It may be through a Big Brothers or Big Sisters program. It may be through your church. It may be a neighbor.

Your child needs to hear opinions from other adults who love him. He needs to see how other adults handle various circumstances and situations in life.

**An Exception to the Rule** The only time you should cut off a relationship between your child and another adult is if you suspect that abuse of any type is occurring—physical, sexual, or emotional. In those cases, cut off the relationship definitively. If your child truly is being abused, he will be grateful to you for rescuing him.

If the child is older at the time of the abuse, let your child know why you no longer are giving your permission for him to spend time with the adult in question. If your child truly has been abused, he will thank you and think better of you.

In sharing your child with others, from time to time, talk over with the other adult various problems your child may be having. Get their insights.

Let some visits be spontaneous, others planned. Keep the relationship as normal as possible. For example, don't insist that your child always dress in her best church or party clothes to visit Aunt Lou.

### Maintain Healthy Detachment    Don't attempt to debrief your child after each visit. Express your interest in what your child "got to do" with the other adult, but don't grill your child for details beyond what your child is willing to share. The parent who seeks desperately for information sends a message to the child, "I'm not sure I trust you with this adult. I'm not sure I trust her love for you."

Finally, let your child know that it's OK for him to love someone else. You can say to your child, "I'm glad you have such a good relationship with Gramps." Or, "Isn't it neat that Aunt Karen lives close to us so you can be with her?"

One of the greatest qualities about love is that we human beings can never get enough of the real thing. Share your child with others so that he or she can be *deluged* with a massive, overwhelming, outpouring of love. Your child will love being loved like that!

# 41 ✦ Leave an After-School Love Message for Your Child

Anticipate your child's return after a long day at school. Have a surprise awaiting him. Send the message to your child, "I love being with you. I'm glad you're home!"

Here are some surprises children love:

- *A snack.* I have never met a child who didn't come home from school hungry. Core and cut up an apple. Have half a sandwich ready and waiting, along with a glass of milk. Put out a couple of cookies with a glass of juice.
- *A different kind of treat.* Your message of love may be a new video for your child to play until you get home. It may be a game, an item of clothing that your child has wanted, or an envelope with your child's allowance in it.
- *A note from you.* Stick it on the bathroom mirror: "Glad to see you are at home safe and sound! I'll be home about 5:30 today." Or put a note on the refrigerator door, "There's a piece of cake already cut and wrapped for you as a snack. Not a bite more. Love, Mom."

- *A message on the family answering machine.* Parker leaves a message every day for his son on their answering machine. His son knows to check the machine as soon as he gets home. "Hi, son. This is Dad. I'll be home soon. Get your homework done now so we can play a little catch when I get home. I should be there by six o'clock."

- *A phone call from you.* Carolyn calls her son every day at the time he usually gets home. They talk over the day for a few minutes, and also the family's plans for the evening. Kitt, on the other hand, has her son call her the minute *he* gets home.

In leaving a message for your child, make certain that your instructions are clear. Communicate using words that your child can read. Make certain that you give *all* the details. For example, tell the child precisely what time you expect him to come in from playing basketball, exactly when you'd like for him to put the casserole in the oven and at what temperature (and remind him to turn on the oven), which outfit you want him to change into.

The ideal, of course, is for parents to be at home when their children are at home. In today's world, that isn't always possible. Make sure that your child has a "piece of your presence" even if you can't be there.

# 42 ✦ Help Your Child Build a Collection

A collection, built over time, is a great way of expressing the continuity of your love to your child.

**Sharing Time** Whenever possible, choose collections that can relate to *time* you spend with your child. Make a collection not only something that your child *has,* but something your child *does.* Some possibilities are:

- *A stamp collection.* Accompany your child to stamp stores. Take him to the post office when new issues are available.
- *A book collection.* Don't just give your child an occasional volume. Take your child with you to the bookstore to pick out a new addition to his or her "set."
- *A rock or shell collection.* Collect some samples on your hikes together and purchase other items in specialty shops.

*A collection may have practical use later in life.* In my case, the collection was one of miniature vases. My mother advised that I collect something that I might enjoy even as an adult, and I now often use these little vases for individual blooms around the house or at individual place settings for dinner parties. The vases were acquired as we traveled together rather extensively during my growing-up years.

**Building Memories** Katie has an add-a-pearl necklace that her parents started for her when she was born. The final pearls on the strand were a present to her on the eve of her wedding, so that she might wear a completed necklace with her wedding gown.

Justin's collection of train cars grows in value for him every year. He has a train set that is the envy of his entire neighborhood. Jordan's collection of Christmas ornaments is something she will take with her when she leaves home one day. Linda's collection of clowns now fills an entire shelf in her room. Clowns still make her smile.

A collection says to your child, "My love extends over time. So does your acquiring of these things. My love for you is longstanding. It grows each day. My love is a treasure of exceedingly great value; just as these things become more valuable to you as time passes, so will my love." Children are here-and-now creatures. As children grow, they have a sense of time, history, and continuity. Let a collection be a tangible expression of your love in the context of years.

# 43 ✦ Avail Yourself of Help When Your Child Needs It

Don't think that you need to be all things to your child. Get professional help for your child when he needs it. Most parents readily take their children to physicians, dentists, and optometrists. They know they aren't capable of handling certain health care problems. These same parents, however, are often reluctant to get help in areas where they think they are supposed to have the answers.

**Learning Problems**  Get help when your child needs *tutoring in a school subject*. Don't let your child flounder in a basic subject. If your child isn't reading at grade level or is having trouble with math, get a tutor. Don't let the problem build. I encountered a student in a college classroom one day who stated in a matter-of-fact tone, "I can't do this assignment because I can't do percentages." "OK," I responded. "I'll show you how to figure percentages." "No," she added, "you don't understand. I *can't* do percentages. I've tried for years and I can't *do* them."

This young woman had been "helped" by her father, who, unfortunately, didn't know how to figure percentages either! He had so confused his daughter that he had led her to the conclusion that she was ignorant and totally beyond help in this area of mathematics.

If your child is in tears (or near them) because he or she can't seem to understand a school subject, take tests, or solve a problem—get help. Your child may have received some incorrect or confusing instruction that needs to be undone. Or, he may have a learning disability that needs remediation.

***Behavioral Problems***   If your child has continued and persistent difficulty dealing with anger, appears despondent and talks about death, can't seem to make or sustain friendships, frequently is in trouble at school, or appears increasingly withdrawn—seek out professional help.

You may want to start with a pastor, rabbi, or priest. You may want to start with your child's teacher, principal, or school counselor. They may refer you elsewhere. If they do, follow up on their lead.

Don't assume that your child will just "grow out of it." He may not. Your child may have had an experience that you know nothing about. He may have been abused in some way or have witnessed abuse. She may have experienced a hurt that she can't tell you about, for any one of a hundred reasons. Give your child the opportunity to talk to a professional counselor about the problem.

Encourage your child. Let your child know that you believe things are going to get better for her! Above all, restate your love. Say, *"Honey, I love you and I want to see you experience life to the fullest. I want to see you get the greatest amount of fulfillment and enjoyment out of life. At times we all face problems that seem humongous to us. Usually, we find those problems seem smaller if we get somebody to help us with them."* Don't let your child see therapy as a punishment for her behavior; don't let her regard herself as sick or deficient. Put therapy in the context of learning and helping.

Many times parents assume that love will cover all problems or that love will cure all ailments. That isn't so. Many times a problem is related to depths of grief or guilt or loneliness that love can't resolve by itself. A child's physical chemistry may be out of whack, and the root of a learning or behavioral problem may be physiological more than psychological. Your child may have had an encounter or be experiencing something that is completely foreign to your previous experience.

Get the help your child needs. That is often the way in which love manifests itself with greatest impact. "Mom cared enough to help me through this. Dad loved me enough to recognize my need and to get help in meeting it."

# 44 ✦ Have Something of Your Child's as a Permanent Part of Your Home

*This "simple way" is addressed to those grandparents, aunts and uncles, and godparents who frequently have the children they love over to their homes.* Here is a way for *you* to say "I love you" to a special child in your life.

Have something in your home that is the child's property, exclusively for his use and available to him whenever he comes to visit. It may be a pillow, blanket, or sheets just for the child's use, or a special towel in the bathroom cupboard, or a bottom dresser drawer filled with a variety of toys, games, and puzzles. That sends a message to your beloved child, "Just as you have a special place in my heart, you have a special place in my home."

**Reserved Property** Connie has Mickey Mouse sheets available in her linen closet exclusively for the use of her young grandson, Thompson, who comes to spend the night at least once a month. The sheets not only have become a tradition in Thompson's life, but they are a reminder of a happy day spent with his grandparents at Disneyland.

Make sure your child's special items don't go home with your child. This does not mean, of course, that you can't give your child items to take home. A collection of pretty leaves gathered from your autumn-laced sidewalk, flowers from your garden, a batch of homemade cookies, the T-shirt you've painted together. Let your child take away the temporary remembrances of his or her visit.

**Special Necessities** Have a toothbrush, baby shampoo, and a bottle of bubble bath available exclusively for your child's use. As your child grows into a teen, update the shampoo and add a razor. Your teen will still need a toothbrush and enjoy a bottle of bubble bath or bath salts.

Keep his or her favorite cereal in an airtight plastic container in the cupboard. That goes for all ages. Have a bathrobe and slippers just for your child's use. Keep a nightgown or pajamas at your house for the spur-of-the-moment overnight visit.

Let your child know, "I've planned for you in my life. I want you always to feel comfortable here. I want this to be your home-away-from-home."

# 45 ✦ Set Rules

Children need and want rules. They need rules for their safety and protection. They also need to know that you are *concerned* with their safety and protection. In spite of what they may say in a moment of anger or frustration, a child regards rules as a sign that you care. Rules say to your child, "I love you enough to care what happens to you. I love you enough to protect you."

When you give your child rules you are not only setting boundaries beyond which they may not go, but you are establishing an area in which they may move with a great deal of freedom. In defining for your child what is off-limits, you are also establishing what is permissible.

Place your emphasis on the positive side of the boundary line when you give rules to your child. Instead of saying, "You may not leave the upper floor of the mall," try saying, "You may go into any store you choose on the upper floor. But, don't go to any other floor before we talk about it."

Here are three guidelines for setting rules:

- Don't let your child engage in any activity that has a high percentage of likelihood for physical or emotional harm.

- Don't let your child willfully destroy property.
- Don't let your child willfully hurt another person.

Sometimes you may want to couch rules in terms of their being "house rules." In other words, let your child know that while certain rules are not the law of the land or principles by which the cosmos operates, they *are* rules that you've decided to have for your house and for your family.

As a parent, making rules *is* your prerogative. Let your child know that you have the privilege of making rules. As long as you have responsibility for your child, you have the right to make rules for his behavior and to require that he keep them.

**Use Your Instinct**   Still other rules are what a friend of mine terms "instinct rules." Rules tend to govern generalities. Children tend to deal in specifics. Applying general rules to specific situations often comes down to "instinct." You can always say to your child, "My instinct as a father tells me this is one time when I should say no." Or, "I know your regular curfew is eleven o'clock. And yes, it's true that on a few occasions I've let you extend that to midnight. But this time the eleven o'clock rule needs to stand. And no, I don't have any other reason than that I have a feeling that you should be in by eleven."

You don't need to explain all of your rules to your child. Some you will want to explain. Explain what you feel needs to be known or that which a child can understand. It is your privilege as a parent, however, to require obedience even without an explanation. Let your child know up front that "just because I said so" *is* an acceptable answer in many situations.

**Be Consistent**    The most important aspect of a rule is its consistent application. Don't switch rules in the middle of the stream. Let Monday's rule also be Tuesday's rule. Also, be consistent in your rules for all your children. Don't have one set of rules for the boys and another for the girls.

Rules need to flow from a consistent value system. If it is wrong to lie to parents, it also should be wrong to lie to a brother or sister. If it is wrong to cheat on a test, it also should be wrong to cheat when you are counting out Monopoly money to your friends.

**Be Sensitive to Your Child**    Be aware that in many cases your child wants you to say no. He doesn't want to be responsible for a yes decision. The movie is guaranteed to frighten every viewer out of his wits. All the other kids are going. Your child pleads with you in their presence for permission to go. You say, "No." Don't be surprised if your child appears relieved.

Be sensitive to an adjustment of rules as your child grows up. The rule of lights out at eight o'clock is not going to be pertinent to a twelve-year-old.

Rules imply a set of punishments. There has to be an "if" clause for most rules to have impact. *"If you leave the yard, you will have to come into the house and stay inside for the rest of the afternoon." "If you hit Marsha again, accidentally or not, you will have a ten-minute 'time out' when we get home."*

Always, always, *always* state rules in terms that children understand. Use simple, concise language. Spell out consequences clearly.

Be prepared to restate and restate and restate your position. Tuesday's rule may be Monday's rule, but your child may not remember it was a rule or that it is Tuesday! As my friend Charles once said to me, "Most of parenting seems to come down to one word: repetition."

Follow through on punishments when your established rules are disobeyed. Don't make idle threats. Let your child know that when you say something, you mean it. Let your child know that your decision is final and not subject to negotiation. That way, your child will be more likely to believe you when you say, "I love you!"

# 46 ✦ Pray for Your Child

Earlier in this book, we provided suggestions for praying with your child. Another way to love your child is to pray *for* your child.

*Prayer does something within your own heart.* It enlarges your capacity to feel love for your child. It brings things to your conscious mind that may have been lingering in your subconscious. It provides an avenue for you to forgive yourself for times when you know that you have failed your child as a loving parent.

Sabrina often goes into her son's room to pray for him while he is away at school. There in the midst of all his "junk," surrounded by the environment he has created largely for himself, she will lie on his bed and attempt to see the world as her son sees it. "I get a much better sense of what he values and what he's facing," she says. "It's as if I'm truly 'walking a mile in his moccasins.'"

## Occasions for Prayer

- Pray for your child before you punish your child. Ask God for guidance, temperance, and patience.

- Pray for wisdom that you might help your child confront life's problems and that you might train your child in the best ways possible.
- Pray for forgiveness for those times when you know that you've let your child down in some way.
- Pray for a solution to your child's problems. It may be a behavioral problem, a health problem, a school problem.
- Pray for the ability to show more love to your child.
- Pray a blessing on your child. Ask God for an abundant outpouring of opportunities and good things into your child's life, both now and in the future.

You'll find that prayer brings your relationship with your child into sharper focus, that you have more patience and insight into your child's life, and that you have an added sense of strength as a parent.

*Your child will know you are praying for him.* There will be times when he overhears you and you aren't even aware of it. There will be times when he wants you to pray for him in his presence, especially if he is sick or facing a challenge of some type.

Let your child know that you are praying for him. Ask him, from time to time (or even daily) if there is something in his life about which he would like for you to pray.

***A Bedtime Ritual***   Jim sometimes found it difficult to talk to his children face to face about serious matters. In fact, Jim didn't talk much at all in the presence of his family members. All of his life he had been classified as shy or reserved. It was a fact his wife and children accepted.

Instead of carrying on conversations with his children, Jim had a habit of going into their rooms after they were asleep, and there, staring over the side of the crib or sitting on the edge of the bed, he would pray for his children, one by one. He would tell them how he felt, and what he hoped for them. He would pray for their future and their success in life.

Pray for your child in his presence:

- When your child is sick. Let him know that you believe he is going to get well.
- When your child is lonely or sad. Let him know that you believe he's going to have bright moments ahead.
- When your child is facing a real challenge— moral, academic, athletic, spiritual. Let your child know that you believe he is going to stand strong and come through this challenge victoriously and that even if he doesn't win, he can still be a "winner."

Nobody truly understands how prayer works. But nearly everybody can attest to a time when a prayer was answered. Prayer fills in the gaps that you may feel in your relationship with your child.

# 47 ✦ Don't Forget the Little Touches

Let your relationship with your child be filled with easygoing, not-too-serious, little touches.

Give him a little shoulder hug as you stand in the supermarket check-out line, hold her hand for just thirty seconds as you walk from the car into church, squeeze his hand after a blessing is asked before the evening meal.

**Parting Rituals Help** Brad absolutely refused to let his mother hug or kiss him goodbye as he left for school. "What if the guys see you?" he would say. "They'd think I'm a sissy." Instead, Brad and his mother share "elbow kisses." As Brad leaves in the morning, he puts out his elbow toward his mother, she puts out hers, and for just a second or two, they touch elbows. Subtle. Not too mushy. But a little touch that marks every day.

Jeremy's mother drives him to school each day. Their parting ritual is similar. Mom simply reaches over and squeezes his knee three times. "One for me, one for Dad, and one for God." Jeremy feels three times loved.

Marlene and her mother hold fingers. "When Marlene was just a toddler, she'd reach up and grab hold of my little finger. She didn't want me to hold her hand—I think that was too much of *my* holding *her* hand. Instead, she wanted the independence she felt in grasping *my* finger at will. Sometimes when we are standing in church together now (and she's already to my shoulder, you realize), I'll still find her reaching over to link her little finger with mine."

Grandfather offers his arm to Mindy as a gallant gesture every time they walk together. Mindy feels special as "Grandfather's girl." (Grandfather also feels more secure in walking.)

**Little Touches Mean a Lot**   What do these moments of touching do for your child?

- They remind him of your presence. A small touch can be reassuring to a child just before he goes on stage, or as he comes or goes from your presence. If a child is standing close enough to you for you to touch him, consider him within touching range.
- Little touches remind your child that you think she is *worthy* of your touch, that you want to be close to her, and that you enjoy her company.
- Little touches communicate, *"Thanks, honey."* Or, *"Way to go."* Or, *"You can do it."* And always, *"I love you."*

Don't make them a major production. Keep them as *little* touches, a layer of icing on the rich cake of your love!

# 48 ✦ Let Your Child Know He Can Hurt You

When your child hurts your feelings, willfully or unknowingly, let your child know that you have been hurt. Find a moment when the two of you are alone and say, *"Honey, you remember when you said or did, or didn't do . . . well, that hurt me."*

Your child is likely to sense that you have been hurt, although he may not define it as hurt. He may think you are angry, upset, frustrated, or annoyed. By telling your child you have been hurt, you teach him to understand your feelings and to be more sensitive to various signals from others in the future.

Telling your child that you have been hurt gives your child an opportunity to ask your forgiveness. He may not use words, he may just be kinder to you for a few days or show up with a flower or write you a little note. Accept your child's acts of repentance.

Legitimate hurts which you should discuss with your child include any incident when your child shows disrespect for you:

- Insults (public or private).
- Cursing or name-calling, at you or about you.

- Lies told about you.
- Blatant and willful rejection.
- Nagging criticism.

In some cases, your child's behavior may warrant punishment from you. How can you tell when punishment is warranted? Any time your child does something to you that you don't want your child to do to any other adult, including his or her own spouse someday.

In cases where you decide punishment is necessary, let your child know plainly *before* you punish him, *"I've been very hurt by what you've just done or said, but that is not the reason that I'm punishing you. I'm punishing you because that is not an acceptable way to treat any adult, including me. I don't want you ever to do that again. This punishment is to help you remember not to repeat such behavior."*

Draw a distinction between your personal hurt and your parental role as the punishment-giver. Assure your child that, in spite of your hurt feelings, your love for him remains strong.

**Positive Messages**    What messages are sent to your child when you let him know that he can, and has, hurt you?

*First, he will learn that your love is resilient. It can survive injury and insult.* It can last through rejection. It can endure beyond criticism. *"My love for you, honey, is stronger than anything you can throw up against it."*

*Second, she will learn that loving relationships are not marked by insult, hurt, criticism, or lies.* Instead, the hallmarks of loving relationships are praise, giving, blessing, helping, and truth.

*Third, your child will learn that his actions can wound and that he is responsible for the wounds he inflicts on others.* Children often see adults as impervious to hurt. (They often see God in this way, too.) Letting your child know that you are vulnerable makes your child more sensitive to the fact that all human beings have feelings that can be injured.

**Emotional Growth** Many children grow up thinking, "It's not my fault if another person feels hurt. It's their fault. They shouldn't have felt that way. They should have been able to overlook what I said or should have ignored what I did." That's a self-centered, self-justifying, arrogant attitude that often results in shallow, temporary, unsatisfying, or dysfunctional relationships.

Confront your child with the insults that issue from his mouth. He is just as responsible for what he says as for what he does.

Loving relationships sometimes do have painful moments. Don't deny them. Grow through them. If you didn't love, you wouldn't feel pain. When your child causes you pain, show your child that love can conquer or outlive pain. Show your child just how strong love can be. He'll never know it if he thinks that he can never hurt you.

# 49 ✦ Personalize Your Child's World

Lift up your child's name. Let him know that you consider his name, the nearest and dearest representations of himself beyond his own physical body, to be valuable beyond measure. You will be sending a loud and clear message to your child, "I count you as special. I love you as I love no other."

Encourage your child to stick his hands and feet into the wet cement poured adjacent to your new swimming pool. Date it. Give your child the thrill of knowing that he has made a lasting mark on your home.

Monogram a couple of your teen's long-sleeved dress shirts. It only costs a few dollars at a tailor shop. Send the message to your child that he is special and that you consider him a cut above the norm.

**Personalize Your Child's Room**  Have a nameplate made for your child's room. It might be an engraved brass door knocker for the door into his room. It might be a name carved out of wood. It might be a needlework nameplate. Let your child know with assurity: "This is my space. My name and my space are important to Mom and Dad."

Frame certificates for your child's room in which

his name is associated with a good deed. Show his trophies. Does your child fail to win trophies or bring home certificates? Then make up one for him. Buy one for him. It can be a certificate awarded to "The Greatest Daughter in the World" or for "Superior Performance as a Son." Trophy shops have all sorts of toppers and styles. I recently saw a trophy in the room of a thirteen-year-old boy that read, "Grandpa's Favorite Fishing Companion—Summer 1988" above the child's name.

How about ordering a monogrammed pin for your teenage daughter or having her first initial engraved on a locket? How about monogramming a beach towel or oversized bath towel for your son?

## More Personal Touches

- Buy a mug with your child's initial on it.
- Put her initials on a diary or journaling book.
- Have your child's initials put on his first leather wallet.
- Buy a keychain with your child's initial after she gets her first driver's license.

These added touches tell your child, "You are unique. Even if someone else in the world has your name, nobody else by that name is *my* child. And, nobody else receives the same love that I have in my heart for you."

# 50 ✦ Take Time for Yourself

Be good to yourself. Pamper yourself occasionally. Send a signal to your child that you like yourself. The more valuable you consider yourself to be, the more valuable are your expressions of love to your child.

Do you think of yourself as being important? You are! You are your child's parent. That's important. Hold your head up and declare to yourself in the mirror, "I have an important role to fill on this earth." Let your child sense the feeling, "I'm loved by an important person."

Do you think of yourself as being beautiful? You are to your child. Nothing is more beautiful than the touch of your hands, your smile, the twinkle in your eye, and your arms wrapped around your child in a bear hug. Send a message to your child that she is adored by a wonderful, lovely person.

Respect yourself. Your child will not only have greater respect for you, but also greater respect for the love you share.

***Love Yourself***   Make it a habit to get dressed, comb your hair, and put on your makeup before your child leaves the house in the morning. Shut yourself away from time to time to take a long bubble bath.

Simply say to your child, "Excuse me while I take a moment for luxury. You know the house rules. Keep them."

Dress up for dinner occasionally, and insist that your children dress up, too. This is especially important if your spouse comes home dressed in a suit—and perhaps, heels!

**Share It with Your Child**   Share your accomplishments with your child, too. Let your child know when you win an award, receive praise from a supervisor, or are pleased within yourself at the good job you've done on a project. *"It was a smashing dinner, if I do say so myself!" "It was first-rate work, whether the big boss ever sees it or not."*

Occasionally declare a household naptime or quiet hour. If your child complains that he isn't sleepy, let him curl up on his bed with a book. Instruct him, *"Don't awaken me, and don't leave your room!"* Let your child know that you deserve a little time and space to call your own, including an occasional nap.

Enjoy the purchase of a new dress, suit, or pair of shoes. Delight in gifts of fragrance and personal items. Let your child know that you value your own body, your appearance, your accomplishments.

The more your child senses that you value yourself, the greater the value your child will place upon you. And the greater he will value your expressions of love.

# 51 ✦ Protect Your Child

As a parent, you are your child's foremost protector. Parents often have a good understanding of that when their children are young. *"Don't run into the street." "Don't touch the hot stove." "Don't talk to strangers."* The responsibility increases, however, rather than decreases as your child grows older.

- *Protect your child from physical danger.* Make sure your child knows when and how to make an emergency call. Make certain your child knows his name, address, phone number, your name, and your phone number at work. Prepare your child for encounters with strangers. *"If anybody offers you anything that sounds too good to be true, run like crazy and come tell me about it!"*

  Rehearse fire drills with your child in your own home. Teach your child what to do if he gets lost. Give your child swimming lessons. Teach your child basic first-aid skills. Above all, make sure your child *feels* safe in his own home. You may need to add another lock to the back door.

- *Protect your child from drugs.* Give him the information he needs, and give it to him before anybody else does. Arm yourself with facts. Explain the difference between medicines and illegal drugs to your child. Let your child know that drugs abuse people and take control of their lives.

- *Protect your child from an unwanted pregnancy.* Talk to your child about sex before anybody else does. Explain how both the male and female bodies function. Talk about appropriate behaviors between boys and girls, men and women, according to your value system. Don't just say, "Don't." Tell your child why. Discuss precautions, prevention, and abstinence. Explode the myths that your child is likely to hear about sex. Say to your child, *"I love you so much that I want you to experience all of the right kinds of love at the right time and in the right ways."*

- *Protect your child's mind.* Don't allow pornography in your home. Watch what your child watches. Do you see occultic signs or practices? (Do you know what to look for? If not, find out.) Do you see violence? Do you see blatant acts of prejudice against race, sex, or nationality? Turn off the message.

  Guide your child's selection of reading material. Regulate your child's attendance at movies. Feed your child's mind as well as you feed your child's body.

- *Protect your child from abuse.* Let your child know that he has a right *not* to be abused physically, emotionally, or sexually. Tell your child in plain terms what is off limits, what is private about his or her body, and how to recognize an emotionally destructive relationship. Reinforce the message to your child, *"I love you and don't want to see you abused in any way."*

Do not allow self-abusive behavior in which a child calls himself a failure, declares that he is inadequate in some way, or inflicts an injury on himself. Assure him you will continue to love him even if he never hits a home run. Tell her you will always love her, even if she never gets her hair to do exactly what she wants it to do. Continually reinforce the message to your child, "I love you for who you are, not for anything that you do or don't do."

- *Protect your child's heart.* Give your child lessons in how to cope with failure or rejection. Teach your child how to stand up on the side of moral right. Give your child a faith to which he can cling in dark, lonely, or frightening moments. Say to your child, *"I love you and I want you to love yourself."*

# 52 ✦ Don't Let Your Child Worship You

This final "simple way" to tell your child "I love you" is really not all that simple. Parents love to be adored. Who wouldn't want to be?

Let your child love you. Enjoy your moments together. Take delight in your child and let her relish life in your presence. But don't let your child worship you.

**Worship Is Different from Love.** Worship is rooted in three basic concepts.

- *The object of worship is incapable of doing any wrong.* The object of true worship has a perfect value system and always executes perfect justice. Stated simply, you don't qualify and never can. You will err. You won't get it right all the time.

- *The object of worship is omniscient* (having infinite wisdom and knowledge), omnipotent (having infinite power, capability, and skill), and omnipresent (infinitely available, always and in each moment). Again, you don't qualify. You won't always be there for your child and even when you

are physically available, your child won't always feel that you're "there" for him emotionally.
- *The object of worship has a perfect love.* As good as your love is for your child, as wonderful and high and wide and glorious, it isn't perfect.

Talk about love to your child. Talk about its limitations and share with your child the fact that loving is sometimes difficult to do, even for the most loving and lovable person on the earth.

**You're Not Perfect**    Again, *don't* let your child worship you. Don't let him set you up in his heart or mind as perfection. Give him a bigger view of perfection. Point him to God. Give him a broader view of love. Allow him to experience it from others. Give him a clearer understanding of how love works—as a means of forgiving failures, overcoming faults, facing up to sins, and healing hurts.

Although you are not worthy of *worship,* you, as a parent, are still the best example of *love* that your child will ever know. Your child can't grow into a healthy adult without your love being made manifest.

You may be a grandparent, an aunt or uncle, a godparent, a teacher, or any adult who loves children. Your love is important to a child, too.

Nobody can give to your special child what you can give. So give of yourself freely and consistently. Be generous with your love, and in your child, love *will* grow.